cooking with
Quinoa

cooking with
Quinoa

50 fabulous recipes making the most of this adaptable and nutritious wonder grain

PENNY DOYLE

Photography by Nicki Dowey

HERMES
HOUSE

To Lee, my husband, and our dear daughters, Emily and Polly, for their support and understanding, and to my inspiring parents, Geoff and Helen for their pride and enthusiasm.

This edition is published by Hermes House, an imprint of Anness Publishing Ltd, Blaby Road, Wigston, Leicestershire LE18 4SE; info@anness.com; www.hermeshouse.com; www.annesspublishing.com

If you like the images in this book and would like to investigate using them for publishing, promotions or advertising, please visit our website www.practicalpictures.com for more information.

Publisher: Joanna Lorenz
Executive Editor: Joanne Rippin
Photographer: Nicki Dowey
Food Stylists: Lucy McKelvie, Jayne Cross, Emma Jane Frost
Props Stylist: Lucy Harvey
Designer: Adelle Mahoney

© Anness Publishing Ltd 2013

PUBLISHER'S NOTE
Although the advice and information in this book are believed to be accurate and true at the time of going to press, neither the authors nor the publisher can accept any legal responsibility or liability for any errors or omissions that may have been made nor for any inaccuracies nor for any loss, harm or injury that comes about from following instructions or advice in this book.

NOTES
Bracketed terms are intended for American readers. For all recipes, quantities are given in both metric and imperial measures and, where appropriate, in standard cups and spoons. Follow one set of measures, but not a mixture, because they are not interchangeable.
Standard spoon and cup measures are level. 1 tsp = 5ml, 1 tbsp = 15ml, 1 cup = 250ml/8fl oz. Australian standard tablespoons are 20ml. Australian readers should use 3 tsp in place of 1 tbsp for measuring small quantities. American pints are 16fl oz/2 cups. American readers should use 20fl oz/2.5 cups in place of 1 pint when measuring liquids. Medium (US large) eggs are used unless otherwise stated. Electric oven temperatures in this book are for conventional ovens. When using a fan oven, the temperature will probably need to be reduced by about 10–20°C/20–40°F. Check with your manufacturer's instruction book for guidance.
The nutritional analysis given for each recipe is calculated per portion (i.e. serving or item), unless otherwise stated. If the recipe gives a range, such as Serves 4–6, then the nutritional analysis will be for the smaller portion size, i.e. 6 servings. The analysis does not include optional ingredients, such as salt added to taste.

GLUTEN-FREE
Recipes listed as gluten-free contain no naturally gluten-containing ingredients eg wheat, rye or barley. However, many manufactured foods eg stock cubes, some yogurts and soy sauce, may contain gluten so you will need to refer to National Coeliac/Celiac guidelines eg Coeliac UK or Celiac Disease Foundation (US) to ensure that you have suitable gluten-free brands where necessary. Pure, uncontaminated oats are tolerated in moderate amounts by most coeliacs/celiacs, but you may wish to seek the advice of your specialist dietician or doctor before you consume oats.

The publishers wish to thank Alamy for use of their images: p6 (top), 10 (bottom); and Corbis p6 (bottom), 7 (top), and 10 (top).

CONTENTS

INTRODUCTION

Quinoa's rise from a unique dietary staple of the South Americans 6,000 years ago to its status as an emerging Western 'superfood', is remarkable. The nutritional superiority of Quinoa (pronounced 'keen-wa') is driving international demand, and productivity has increased by over a third in recent years. Comparable to other starchy staples such as rice or potato, quinoa boasts more protein, healthy fats, calcium, iron and B vitamins than any other food. It is also cholesterol and gluten-free, and has the added benefit of being wholegrain.

In modern kitchens as well as the most prestigious restaurants around the world, chefs and home cooks are discovering the versatility of quinoa in all its forms, while health-conscious athletes and dieticians are becoming converted to its nutritional benefits. Whether used as a grain, rolled, as flour, puffed or as pasta, quinoa is proving a welcome change to carbohydrate staples of pasta, rice, potatoes and cous cous in family eating. With its distinctive texture, bite and striking colour of the red and black strains, as well as its wide variety of uses, this can only continue.

This collection of 50 inspiring recipes brings vibrant tastes and flavour combinations from around the world to create tempting and delicious dishes, which are full of superfood nutrition. The recipes have been adapted to fit into busy schedules, with ingredients that are widely available. Easy-to-follow instructions take you step by step through all stages of each dish, and the pages are packed with cooking tips, advice, and nutritional information. This book will delight those who are looking for inspiration on how to maximize their use of quinoa, as well as converting those who have yet to discover the Inca's 'mother of all grains'.

Penny Doyle

A FASCINATING HISTORY

Above: A field of ripening quinoa in the Peruvian Andes, where the crop was first grown by the Incas.

Right: Much of the world's quinoa is now grown in Bolivia, and thrives in the high, extremely dry elevations where even grass won't grow.

Below: Colourful sacks of harvested quinoa stand ready for collection, and eventual export, in Challapata, Bolivia.

The quinoa we buy today is the seed of the plant Chenopodium quino. It is classified by some nutritionists as a 'pseudograin' because it contains a similar nutritional profile and cooking properties to other grains, though technically is still a seed. Quinoa is related to Swiss chard, spinach and beetroot, and has been cultivated to produce different coloured seeds such as red, yellow, purple or black, but most widely available and less costly is 'pearl', a pale cream colour.

FOOD OF THE INCAS

Native to the Altiplano people of South America, who started cultivating it over 6,000 years ago, quinoa was an esteemed food of the Incas who used it as a staple cereal in beer and bread. It was considered such a valuable part of the diet in areas of the Andean mountains, where agriculture was challenged by altitude and temperatures, that it was more precious than gold, and many believed it had spiritual properties. The Incas referred to it as *la chisiya mama* (the mother grain), as they thought it also gave longevity.

Quinoa was particularly valued as food for Inca warriors, who had to travel around the large Incan Empire by marching for weeks at high altitudes, without access to meat or vegetation. Quinoa provided crucial stamina and endurance, and was often eaten mixed with fat in the form of 'warballs'.

Recognizing its power, quinoa was unsuccessfully targeted for destruction by the Spanish Conquistadors during their invasion in 1500s, when cultivating it was deemed a crime that was punishable by death. The survival of cultivated quinoa was testament to the bravery and ingenuity of the indigenous peoples, who secretly tended plantations high in the Andes, where quinoa evolved to survive harsh climates of drought, frost and intense sunlight, able to grow in temperatures between 18–100°F/-8–38°C. Having proved its enduring resilience during this period, quinoa earned its 'supergrain' status and today enjoys international cultivation. So far, however, growers in other regions are unable

to match the quality of the excellent, light coloured, sweetly delicate seed that comes from the high mountains of South America.

CULTIVATION AND RESEARCH

The United Nations General Assembly declared 2013 as the International Year of Quinoa, in recognition of ancestral practices of the Andean people, who managed to preserve quinoa in its natural state as food for present and future generations. Foreign-aid organizations have helped develop its status in Peru and Bolivia for commercial exportation, but quinoa is now also grown in Colorado, Canada, Europe, Kenya, Northern India and other areas of South America.

There is a growing environmental interest in cultivating quinoa to grow in Europe, and there is also some research into its possible uses by the pharmaceuticals industry. There is a theory that its saponins may assist in the absorption of medication, and may have antibiotic and antifungal properties. The people of the Andes, growing quinoa today, use the saponin-rich water – a by-product of rinsing quinoa – as a crude soap. NASA are also researching if quinoa could be cultivated within spacecraft, as food for astronauts.

Whatever comes from these research projects, there is no doubt that wherever it can be cultivated there will be an enthusiastic market for quinoa as a nutrient-rich superfood.

Below: Raw white quinoa seeds, before processing.

QUINOA: A TRUE SUPERFOOD

Above: Quinoa grows in a field near the village of Circuta in the Oruro province of Bolivia.

Right: The seeds of the quinoa plant have to be milled and washed before they are sold.

The term 'superfood' is justifiably used to describe quinoa, as it can boast an incredible nutritional profile compared to other grains and carbohydrates. Quinoa is also easy to store, transport and cook, and is inexpensive considering its unique range of nutrients.

NUTRIENT PROFILE

Quinoa has hugely impressive health benefits, first realized by the Incas, but now backed up and proven by modern analysis and research. Granted the nutrient status of 'esteemed' and containing a protein content varying between 12 and 20 percent, quinoa contains all nine essential amino acids (the protein building-blocks) including rarer lysine, methionine, cystine and histidine. The latter is considered essential in the development of children, and is believed to help promote healthy pregnancies and enhance breast milk. It was reported that there was visibly more infant malnutrition amongst Inca infants when it was a forbidden food in the colonial period.

On the basis of its amino acid profile alone, quinoa is considered superior to wheat, barley or even the soya bean. Quinoa is universally favoured by athletes, and those in power sports such as body building, as it helps restore and build muscle after training. It is also low in fat, cholesterol-free, and a good

source of fibre, B vitamins and minerals including iron, calcium, copper, manganese, magnesium, chloride and potassium.

Some research claims that quinoa has medical as well as nutritional benefits. It is possible that quinoa is a useful food for headache sufferers as the magnesium may help blood flow in the brain, therefore easing pain. Quinoa's rich natural antioxidants, which act as a natural preservative of the grain, may help lower the risk of some cancers. There is also growing interest in its possible anti-inflammatory properties that may help in management of rheumatoid arthritis.

GLUTEN-FREE

Unlike many grains eg wheat, barley or rye, quinoa doesn't contain gluten, which causes gut problems and malabsorbtion in those diagnosed with coeliac disease. It is therefore a valuable alternative to pasta, cereals and bread for coeliacs, but also for the growing number of people who are gluten intolerant, and feel better on gluten-free diets. The wide range of quinoa products available, and its versatility, adds to its growing appeal.

WHOLEGRAIN

Quinoa also is termed a 'wholegrain' since it contains all three elements of a seed (germ, endosperm and bran). Eating more whole-grains is associated with a lower risk of chronic diseases including heart disease, diabetes and some cancers. Partly because of its wholegrain status, quinoa is also a low Glycaemic Index (GI) food. GI relates to how quickly carbohydrate foods raise your blood sugar levels and how full you may feel after eating them. Low GI foods like quinoa, sweet potato and granary bread keep you feeling fuller for longer than higher GI foods like mashed potato and white bread.

HIGH FIBRE

Fibre, while technically not a nutrient because most of it is undigested, is essential to the health and functioning of our digestive systems, and can be soluble or insoluble. Quinoa is a high-fibre food with the dual benefits of both soluble (a third) and insoluble fibre (two thirds). Insoluble fibre is undigested by the gut and vital for preventing constipation, haemorrhoids, and gut-related diseases including cancer. Soluble fibre keeps cholesterol levels lower by helping to block its absorption from food. It may also help lower blood pressure and other unhealthy fats in our blood. Fibre-rich foods also help improve the sensitivity of insulin, which may lower the growing incidences of Type II diabetes.

As a fibre-rich food alone, quinoa can significantly help with the reduction of gut-related and other diseases, but when this is added to its other amazing health-packed nutritional benefits, it is clear that quinoa really does qualify as a superfood.

Top: A head of seeds on the quinoa plant.

Above: A bowl of processed and washed quinoa seeds, ready for cooking.

NUTRITIONAL COMPARISON

Average Portion (All grains = 1 cup)	Energy (Kcalories)	Protein (grams)	Carbohydrate (grams)	Fat (grams)	Fibre (grams)	Calcium (mg)	Iron (mg)	Gluten Free	Wholegrain	Glycaemic Index
Quinoa (185g cooked)	222	8	39	4	5	31	3	Yes	Yes	53
Brown Rice (195g cooked)	218	5	45	2	3.5	20	1	Yes	Yes	50
Macaroni (140g cooked)	221	8	43	1	3	10	1	No	No	47
Wholewheat Bread (1 large slice)	104	5	17	1.4	3	45	1	No	Yes	65–70
Baked Potato (medium with skin)	161	4	37	Trace	4	26	2	Yes	No	60
Cous Cous (157g cooked)	176	6	36	Trace	2	13	1	No	No	65
Bulgar (182g cooked)	151	6	34	0.5	8	18	2	No	Yes	48
Egg Noodles (160g cooked)	221	7	40	3	2	19	1	No	N	61

Source: USDA National Agriculture Library - Nutrient Data Laboratory (Online)

KNOW YOUR QUINOA: A DIVERSE SEED

Above: A bowl of cooked quinoa has a multitude of uses in salads, as a side dish, or stirred into soups and stews for added bulk.

Clockwise from top left: Pearl or white quinoa, the most often used type. Red quinoa, with a little extra bite. Tricolour quinoa, a mix of all three colours. Black quinoa, which often adds a dynamic colour contrast to a dish.

Quinoa is available in a few different forms, which makes its use in the kitchen much more versatile. Large supermarkets more and more frequently stock pearl quinoa, but you can also find red and black quinoa online or at health stores, as well as quinoa flakes, pasta, quinoa pops or flour. As demand for quinoa increases, however, so will its availability. Taking the time to ask for quinoa, in all its forms, from supermarkets and local food stores can only increase awareness and help drive demand locally.

TYPES OF QUINOA

Pearl Quinoa
The creamy white grains of quinoa are the most widely available type. It can be used in savoury dishes instead of other carbohydrates, in salads either as a cooked grain or sprouted, and in breakfast cereals and desserts. It has a light, fluffy texture when cooked, and a slightly nutty flavour.

Red Quinoa
This is usually less available and more expensive. It can be used in the same way as pearl quinoa but has a vibrant orange-brown colour, a slightly firmer texture and a nuttier flavour when cooked. It is wonderful for creating drama in dishes on its own or mixed with different coloured quinoa.

Black Quinoa
This is the firmest of the quinoa seeds, having almost a 'crunch' even when cooked. Use as for pearl or red quinoa, or mix them for a vibrant visual effect.

Tricolour Quinoa
This a commerical mix usually of red, black and pearl quinoa, which makes very pretty dishes, particularly salads. The black quinoa usually means the cooked result retains some 'bite', which helps create a contrast of texture. You can, of course, mix your own.

Quinoa Flour
A textured, gluten-free flour that is available from health stores or online. It is easy to make yourself by grinding raw quinoa in a food processor. Quinoa flour is used as a thickener in sauces, in baking breads, cakes, cookies and pastry, and even in desserts. It is best stored in the refrigerator for freshness.

Clockwise from top left:
Quinoa flour, quinoa flakes,
quinoa pasta and quinoa pops.

Quinoa Flakes

These flakes are quinoa seeds that have been rolled, a similar process to porridge oats, and used in the same way. Substitute quinoa flakes for oats in porridge, muesli, granola, crumbles or baking. They retain a slightly firmer texture than oats when cooked.

Quinoa Pops

These are puffed quinoa seeds that look like much smaller puffed wheat. They are available from online suppliers.

Quinoa Pasta

This pasta may be made entirely with quinoa flour, or a mixture of quinoa and rice flours. It is cooked in the same way as regular pasta, and tastes very similar. It can be sourced locally or though online suppliers.

Quinoa Sprouts

These are sprouted quinoa seeds made by storing soaked, damp quinoa in a dark place for a few hours, and are a way of adding extra crunch, texture and nutrients to salads and sandwiches. See page 19 for a detailed method.

Quinoa Greens

The broad leaves of Chenopodium quinoa plants can be eaten as a leaf vegetable or salad, similar to amaranth, but commercial availability is limited to areas where quinoa naturally thrives in dry, high altitudes. For this reason they have not been included in the following recipes, but could be lightly steamed, or tossed and dressed with other salad leaves.

COOKING WITH QUINOA

The relatively small size of this 'pseudo grain' means it takes less time to cook than other comparable grains such as rice, barley or buckwheat, and makes nearly three times its volume after absorbing cooking liquid. After cooking, it develops a fluffy texture and pretty little white 'curls (the cooked germ) that adds to its quirkiness. Quinoa should be 'al dente' with a little bit of bite, but cooking time can of course be adjusted to suit the dish it is to be used in, or to meet personal taste.

Above: Rinsing raw quinoa in water and rubbing it ensures that all the bitter-tasting saponins are removed.

REMOVING SAPONINS

The main difference in preparing quinoa, compared to rice or other grains, is that quinoa needs rinsing in water before cooking, to remove natural 'saponins' that coat the seed. Saponins contribute to the natural hardiness and historical resilience of quinoa as they act as natural pesticides during cultivation. This is a huge economical advantage as it helps to keep costs down by protecting the crop from birds and insects.

Unfortunately saponins have a bitter taste, but this can easily be removed by rinsing. Most commercial quinoa is already rinsed, but it's likely some saponins will remain. Simply running water through quinoa in a sieve or colander, and rubbing it with your fingers, will remove any residues. Once rinsed, there are several ways that you can cook quinoa.

SIMMER AND ABSORB

1 Rinse the quinoa in water. Add 1 part quinoa to 2 parts water in a pan. Bring to the boil, cover and simmer for 14–16 minutes until all of the water is absorbed. There is no need to stir.

2 Set aside the quinoa in the pan, covered and off the heat, for up to a further 10 minutes if a plumper texture is required. Little water should remain, but drain off any excess, particularly so with red or black quinoa.

BOIL AND DRAIN

1 This is a good method for removing excess saponins. Rinse the quinoa and add to a large pan of boiling water (1 part quinoa to 4 parts water approximately).

2 Bring to the boil and simmer, uncovered, for about 15 minutes until the quinoa is plump and fluffy, then drain and serve.

STEAMING

Rinse the quinoa. Follow the manufacturer's instructions for cooking white rice in an electric, hob or microwave steamer, but remember that quinoa will expand to twice its uncooked volume, so allow space for this.

SLOW COOKING

1 Rinse the quinoa, and using a slow cooker, follow the manufacturer's instructions for cooking white rice.

2 Or add quinoa to soups and casseroles, using 1 part quinoa to 2 parts stock. Serve soon after cooking to prevent the quinoa absorbing all of the stock.

BAKING

Place the quinoa with stock or water (1 part quinoa to 2 parts water/stock) in a casserole dish, cover and bake in the oven at 350°F/180°C/Gas 4 for 30–35 minutes.

DRY ROASTING

1 Rinse and pat dry the quinoa. Spread it on a large, ungreased baking sheet

2 Bake at 180°C/350°F/Gas 4 for 25–35 minutes until golden and crunchy. Cool completely then store in an airtight container. Use in granola, or as a topping for salads, mixed with other toasted nuts or seeds.

USING COOKED QUINOA

The table below will help you to calculate how to cook the correct amount of quinoa for our recipes, some of which use cooked quinoa as a starting point. Remember if you are using more concentrated fluids to cook quinoa, such as milk or fruit juice in puddings or porridges, higher volumes of fluid will be needed to help the quinoa cook until tender. As a rule of thumb add an extra 25%, for example 1 part quinoa to 2.5 parts milk/fruit juice/syrup, but be ready to add a little more.

STORING QUINOA

Quinoa's high polyunsaturated fat content means it degrade quickly unless stored in a cool place. At home this means a dark cupboard, in an airtight container. Quinoa flour, with a higher fat content, is best kept in an airtight container in the refrigerator.

Quinoa 'pops' are puffed seeds that can be used in baking, mueslis or granola, and should be stored in an airtight container.

Cooked quinoa should be kept in the refrigerator, covered, and used within a week. It can also be frozen and stored in a plastic or glass tub, or freezer bags, and kept in the freezer for convenient use as needed.

You can add the frozen quinoa straight to recipes, as it scoops out easily from tubs or bags, and will quickly defrost in heated foods like casseroles or soups.

Bulk cooking and storing of quinoa in this way is very efficient use of time and cooking fuel. However, if you are preparing a cold dish or salad using frozen quinoa, it is better to defrost it for 2 hours at room temperature beforehand.

COOKING QUANTITIES

This table shows you how to achieve the required yield of cooked quinoa used in some of the following recipes. As a rule of thumb:

1 part quinoa + 2 parts water/stock = 3 parts cooked quinoa

Note: 1 cup raw quinoa = 190g = 6^{1}/$_2$oz; 1 cup cooked quinoa = 165g = 5^{1}/$_2$oz

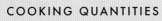

Raw Quinoa	Water	Cooked Quinoa Yield
40g/1^{1}/$_2$oz/^{1}/$_4$ cup	125ml/4fl oz/^{1}/$_2$ cup	125g/4^{1}/$_2$oz/^{3}/$_4$ cup
50g/2oz/^{1}/$_3$ cup	160ml/5fl oz/^{2}/$_3$ cup	190g/6^{1}/$_2$oz/1 cup
75g/3oz/^{1}/$_2$ cup	250ml/8fl oz/1 cup	275g/10oz/1^{1}/$_2$ cups
95g/3.5oz/^{2}/$_3$ cup	320ml/11fl oz/1^{1}/$_3$ cup	375g/13oz/2 cups
115g/4oz/^{3}/$_4$ cup	360ml/12fl oz/1^{1}/$_2$ cups	440g/15^{1}/$_2$oz/2^{1}/$_4$ cups
165g/5.5oz/1 cup	500ml/16fl oz/2 cups	560g/1lb 4oz/3 cups

BEING CREATIVE WITH QUINOA

You'll see from the recipes in this book that quinoa can be incorporated into classic dishes from around the globe, adding colour, texture and flavour that give the recipes a new dimension. Both the grain and flour are useful as thickening agents in stews, soups, casseroles, breads, baked dishes and desserts. The higher fat content of the flour lends itself to delicious baking, with crisp results and an attractive golden colour.

Right: When cooked in milk, quinoa flakes produce a lovely creamy porridge.

Right: Quinoa flour is a great gluten-free substitute for wheat flour in baking.

Quinoa flakes have similar properties to rolled oats, swelling and releasing soluble fibre that gives porridge its texture, making filling breakfasts (muesli, granola, and bars), and helping to keep blood cholesterol levels lower. Puffed quinoa pops are tasty in cereals and can be added to tasty bars. I've also found quinoa 'crispies' (similar to cornflakes) which were delicious covered in chocolate and mixed with chopped apricots, as quick and easy no-bake crispy cakes.

The following basic guidelines will give you ideas for incorporating quinoa into your favourite everyday recipes and benefiting from quinoa's impressive nutrient 'punch'.

BREAD

You can substitute quinoa flour for regular 'strong' bread flour in your favourite recipes, but remember that as it is gluten-free, the strength of the dough and therefore its ability to rise will be reduced. Substituting only up to half the amount of strong bread flour, and adding a pinch of Vitamin C to your dough will help to produce a lighter loaf.

You can use both quinoa flour and cooked pearl quinoa in pizza dough, which is a fantastic way to boost the nutrient content of an everyday family favourite. Substitute up to a half of the regular wheat flour with quinoa flour, but remember the gluten content of the dough will be lower so you will get a thinner and crispier result rather than a 'deep pan' base. If using cooked quinoa add ½ cup to every 2 cups of flour, adding more water as necessary to make a pliable, workable dough.

PASTRY

Quinoa's essential fats ensure a delicious, light-textured pastry that can be used for quiches and sweet and savoury pies.

Make pastry using the usual ratio of half fat to flour, but substitute half the flour with quinoa flour, or quinoa flakes for a more coarse texture. Because of its higher fat content and lack of gluten, the end result will be crisp, but the pastry can be very 'short' and crumbly to work with, so needs to be rested in the refrigerator for at least

Far left: Quinoa flakes (foreground) are produced in a similar way to oats (background), and can be used in conjunction or as a substitute in recipes like granola, flapjacks and crumbles.

Left: Quinoa flour is a great gluten-free substitute for wheat flour in baking.

Left: Red, black and pearl quinoa are superb in salads. They can be bought ready-mixed as tricolour quinoa.

30 minutes. Handle and roll it quickly, avoiding excess handling, with plenty of flour.

BAKING

The recipes in this book use quinoa flour, flakes, cooked quinoa and 'pops' in bakes, desserts, breakfast foods and desserts where it makes a very credible contribution to flavour, texture and nutrient content.

Substitute the same weight of quinoa flakes for rolled oats, or quinoa flour for regular flour in your favourite recipes, but add a little more vanilla extract or other flavouring to be sure that the quinoa doesn't dominate. Use quinoa flakes when you can't get hold of quinoa pops but remember to double the weight to take account of pops' low density.

PANCAKES

You will find two pancake recipes in the following chapters, using quinoa flour, but you can also substitute some or all quinoa flour into your pancake recipes for nutritious family meals. It is always better to make pancake batters half an hour in advance of when needed if possible to allow the flour in the starch to swell.

Above: Quinoa flour in baking gives a very crisp result, and is perfect for making cookies.

Right: Quinoa is a nutritious subsitute for rice in risottos, pilaffs and paellas.

Right: Although it needs to be mixed with strong bread flour, quinoa flour can also be used in bread making, and when added to a seedy wholegrain recipe will give a wonderfully sustaining loaf.

Right: Red and black quinoa have a dramatic colour and nutty texture that make them perfect for use in salads.

SAUCES

Make a white 'bechamel' sauce using quinoa flour to replace regular wheat flour. Usual ratios are 1/4 cup flour to 1/4 cup butter to 2 cups milk (making 1 pint), but you can scale up or down as required. Flavour with plenty of salt and pepper, and add mustard, grated cheese or herbs as desired.

RICE DISHES

Quinoa can be substituted for any type of rice to make delicious, 'earthy' risottos, paellas or pilaffs with bite and texture.

To adapt your favourite rice recipe to quinoa use quinoa in the same way you would use basmati or arborio rice, softening it first in oil or butter and then adding the correct quantity of stock, together with meat, fish or vegetables of your choice. Simmer on a gentle heat, uncovered, for 8–10 minutes, until all the liquid has been absorbed. Stirring constantly for a risotto isn't necessary when using quinoa. Red or black quinoa will always give a firmer texture, whereas pearl quinoa will be softer and fluffier.

SALADS

Using different coloured quinoa will give you striking salads that can be complemented by adding an array of different grains, vegetables, fruit, nuts and seeds.

Incorporate homegrown quinoa sprouts for added crunch and texture. Use intensely flavoured dressings of oil, vinegar, fresh herbs, mustard and soy sauce.

STUFFINGS

Cooked quinoa (in any colour) is great in stuffings instead of breadcrumbs and will absorb the rich flavours of any meat or fish that it is cooked with. Blended with herbs, spices and other flavourings, it can also be used to stuff vegetables such as butternut squash, courgettes (zucchini) or mushrooms.

CRISPY COATINGS

Cooked, fluffed pearl quinoa is a handy and effective alternative to breadcrumbs for those seeking a gluten-free substitute, and can be used for crispy fried fish, chicken or vegetables. Wash and pat dry the food and dust with flour, then dip into beaten egg and then coat in seasoned, cooked pearl quinoa. Shallow-fry in medium-hot rapeseed (canola) oil until golden, turning halfway through. Around 150g/5oz/1 cup of cooked quinoa will coat three to four medium fish fillets, or two chicken breasts cut into goujons. You can flavour the cooked quinoa with chilli flakes, herbs and spices of your choice. Serve with dips or mayonnaise and piles of healthy salad.

TEMPURA

Make a batter using 1 cup quinoa, 1 beaten egg, and 1 cup iced soda water (or beer) for savoury dishes. Sift the quinoa into a bowl, make a well in the centre, and blend in the beaten egg and fluid to make a thick, smooth batter which stays crispy when fried. Alternatively blend in a liquidizer.

Deep-fry coated foods in a pan of moderately hot fat for a few minutes until golden, drain on kitchen paper and serve.

Right: Quinoa makes a superb crispy coating for all kinds of quick and easy fried food, such as fish fillets, chicken goujons, fishcakes and fritters. Simply coat first in flour, then in beaten egg, then quinoa.

CULTIVATION IN YOUR KITCHEN: HOW TO GROW QUINOA SPROUTS

Quinoa sprouts are exciting and quick to grow and often produce two sprouts per seed. Sprouting boosts the seeds' natural enzyme and vitamin content and some believe raw food has unique health benefits, although this is certainly not proven.

1 Rinse the quinoa well in a sieve, rubbing with your fingers to remove the natural saponin coating. Cover in 2cm/1in water and leave for an hour.

2 Thoroughly drain off the excess water in a colander or sieve, shaking very well. They should be damp not drenched.

3 Place the drained sprouts in a thin layer over a the base of a shallow dish.

4 Cover with a clean dish towel and place in a cool, dark place for 10–12 hours.

5 Repeat the rinsing, spreading and covering process two or three times. Sprouts grow to approximately three times the quinoa's original volume and need a day or two to get to a reasonable size.

6 Once fully sprouted, store for up to 3 days in a refrigerator in a sealed container; don't use them if they wilt or brown.

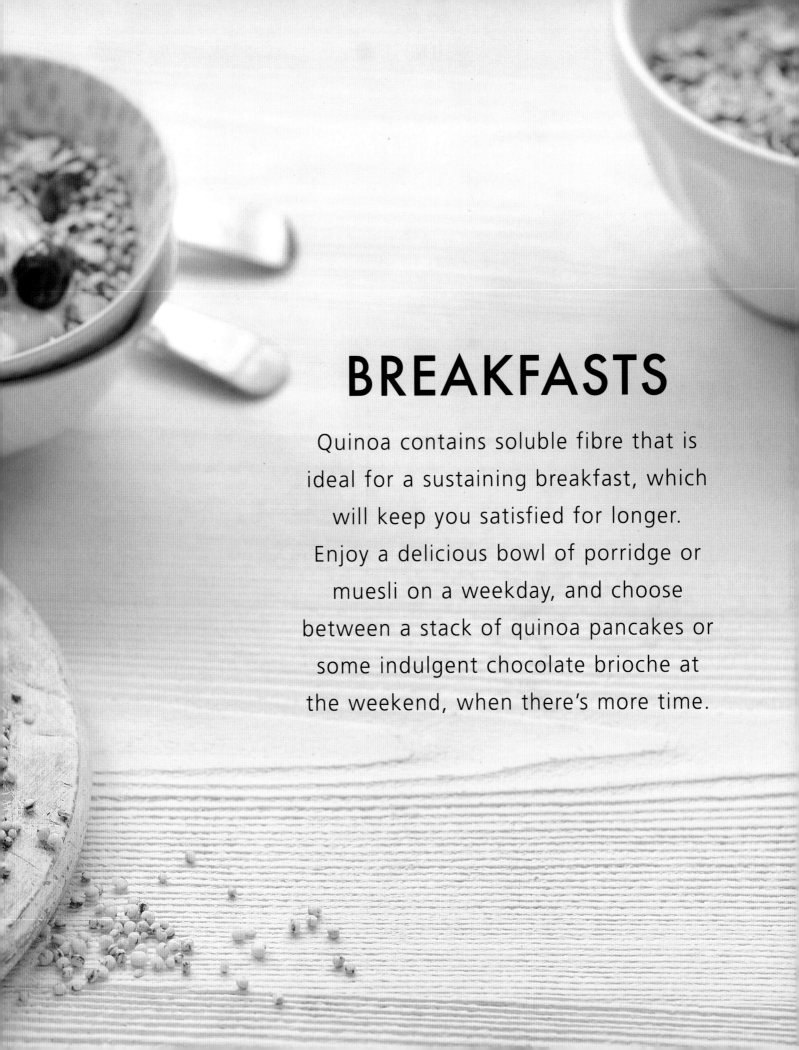

BREAKFASTS

Quinoa contains soluble fibre that is ideal for a sustaining breakfast, which will keep you satisfied for longer. Enjoy a delicious bowl of porridge or muesli on a weekday, and choose between a stack of quinoa pancakes or some indulgent chocolate brioche at the weekend, when there's more time.

Vibrant pink pomegranate – rich in fibre, potassium and vitamin C – looks wonderful stirred into this caramel-coloured porridge. Molasses syrup, a by-product of sugar production, provides precious calcium and iron, but may need sweetening with a drizzle of honey. For convenience it is possible to buy pomegranate seeds ready prepared.

POMEGRANATE AND MOLASSES PORRIDGE

SERVES 4

125g/4¼oz/¾ cup quinoa
250ml/8fl oz/1 cup boiling water
300ml/½ pint/1¼ cups milk
60ml/4 tbsp molasses syrup
clear honey, to taste
150g/5oz pomegranate seeds

1 Put the quinoa in a sieve (strainer) and rinse under cold running water.

2 Transfer the rinsed quinoa to a pan, then add the boiling water and milk. You can use cold water instead of boiling water, if you prefer, but the quinoa will take longer to cook.

3 Simmer the quinoa for 15 minutes, until soft. Stir in the molasses and sweeten with honey as required.

4 Remove from the heat and stir in the pomegranate seeds. Serve drizzled with a little more honey, if you wish.

Nutritional Information: Gluten Free
Energy 238kcal/1002kJ; Protein 7g; Carbohydrate 44g, of which sugars 24g; Fat 5g, of which saturates 2g; Cholesterol 10mg; Calcium 144mg; Fibre 2g; Sodium 44mg.

Prepared with a mixture of quinoa flakes and rolled oats, this porridge is quick and easy to prepare. Adding frozen mixed berries helps deliver a crucial boost of vitamin C and antioxidants during winter months when fresh berries, if available, are more expensive. Most people with coeliac disease can eat oats, so this porridge is useful for them too.

QUICK MIXED BERRY PORRIDGE

SERVES 4–6

600ml/1 pint/2½ cups milk
115g/4oz/1 cup quinoa flakes
50g/2oz/½ cup rolled oats
115g/4oz/1 cup frozen mixed berries
soft light brown sugar or golden (light corn) syrup, to serve

1 Put the milk and quinoa flakes in a pan, bring to the boil and simmer for 5 minutes until the flakes are softened.

2 Add the rolled oats and mixed berries to the pan and simmer for a further 3–5 minutes, until the berries are warmed and the porridge thickened.

3 Serve immediately with soft light brown sugar or golden syrup.

Nutritional Information: Gluten free with GF oats Energy 273kcal/1145kJ; Protein 10g; Carbohydrate 40g, of which sugars 15g; Fat 8g, of which saturates 4g; Cholesterol 19mg; Calcium 209mg; Fibre 4g; Sodium 70mg.

Homemade granola is infinitely more tasty than bought cereal, and you can make it to your own preferences with different quantities of dried fruit, nuts and seeds. Quinoa toasts beautifully in a hot oven, helping to give this granola a lovely crunch that is complemented by a fruit compote. Make double quantities and store in an airtight container.

GRANOLA WITH DATE AND FIG COMPOTE

SERVES 6
175g/6oz/1 cup pearl quinoa, rinsed and drained
50g/2oz/¹/₄ cup butter
60ml/4 tbsp clear honey
5ml/1 tsp ground nutmeg
175g/6oz/1¹/₂ cups quinoa flakes
30ml/2 tbsp flaxseeds (linseeds)
45ml/3 tbsp desiccated (dry unsweetened shredded) coconut
30ml/2 tbsp chopped pistachio nuts
50g/2oz dried banana pieces, chopped into quarters
milk or yogurt, to serve

For the date and fig compote
150g/5oz dried figs, roughly chopped
75g/3oz dried dates, roughly chopped
250ml/8fl oz/1 cup orange juice
2 cloves

1 Dry the rinsed quinoa on kitchen paper or a clean dish towel. Heat the oven to 180°C/350°F/Gas 4. Line a baking tray with baking parchment and spread the quinoa evenly over the base. Bake in the oven for 25–35 minutes until just golden-brown.

2 Meanwhile, place the butter, honey and nutmeg together in a pan and heat gently until the butter melts.

3 Place the quinoa flakes, flaxseeds, coconut, nuts and banana pieces in a large bowl and mix together. Add the melted butter mixture and use the baking parchment to pour in the toasted quinoa, mixing with a wooden spoon.

4 Place the baking parchment back on the baking tray, and spread the granola evenly over the base. Bake for around 20 minutes until golden-brown, removing from the oven before the bananas become too crispy. Set aside to cool completely.

5 For the compote, in a small pan on a low heat, simmer the dried fruit, cloves and orange juice for 8–10 minutes to make a thick, syrupy sauce. Stir regularly to prevent sticking. Remove the cloves. Set the compote aside to cool, then chill.

6 Serve the granola in a bowl topped with a spoonful of compote, adding milk or yogurt as required. The granola will stay fresh for up to a week in an airtight container, and the compote will keep for up to a week in the refrigerator.

COOK'S TIP
Adjust the baking time according to how crispy and golden-brown you like your granola to be, and keep a close eye on it to avoid the dried fruit scorching.

VARIATIONS
Use other fruit, such as dried mango, dried pineapple or plump raisins.

....
Nutritional Information: Gluten free
Energy 468kcal/1962kJ; Protein 11g; Carbohydrate 68g, of which sugars 37g; Fat 18g, of which saturates 8g; Cholesterol 16mg; Calcium 127mg; Fibre 8g; Sodium 101mg.

The great thing about making your own muesli is that you can decide what goes in it and you can tweak the combinations to taste. You could make double the quantity in order to stay well stocked with nutritious breakfasts for the week ahead. This version is gluten-free, but you can swap cornflakes for wheat or barley flakes if you prefer.

MULTIGRAIN QUINOA MUESLI

SERVES 4
50g/2oz/ 1/3 cup hazelnuts
50g/2oz/ 1/4 cup pumpkin seeds
50g/2oz/ 1/2 cup quinoa flakes
25g/1oz/1 cup quinoa 'pops'
50g/2oz/1 cup crisped rice cereal
25g/1oz/ 2/3 cup cornflakes
25g/1oz/ 1/6 cup dried blueberries
25g/1oz/ 1/6 cup dried cranberries
natural (plain) yogurt and honey, or
  milk and fresh fruit, to serve

1 Under a medium grill (broiler), toast the hazelnuts and pumpkin seeds for a few minutes until the seeds start to pop and the nuts are browning. Watch the nuts closely, as it is easy to scorch them.

2 Roughly crush the toasted hazelnuts with the end of a rolling pin. Set aside to cool completely.

3 Mix the cooled nuts and seeds with the remaining ingredients in a large bowl and store in an airtight container. Serve in a bowl, with yogurt and honey, or milk and fresh fruit.

COOK'S TIP
Quinoa pops are puffed quinoa seeds, available in health stores and online.

VARIATION
Change the types of fruit and nuts if you wish. Pecan nuts or sliced almonds combine well with sunflower seeds.

Nutritional Information: Gluten Free
Energy 333kcal/1398kJ; Protein 8g; Carbohydrate 43g, of which sugars 11g; Fat 15g, of which saturates 2g; Cholesterol 0mg; Calcium 94mg; Fibre 0g; Sodium 150mg.

Of Italian origin, frittata is a versatile dish, made more substantial than a French-style omelette by the addition of meat, fish and vegetables. Quinoa can replace the traditional potato, and with a useful amount of watercress and salmon, this makes a hearty one-dish brunch. Any leftovers can be eaten cold in a packed lunch.

SALMON AND QUINOA FRITTATA

SERVES 4
15ml/1 tbsp olive oil
1 medium onion, finely diced
1 orange or red (bell) pepper, chopped
2 cloves garlic, crushed
5ml/1 tsp fennel seeds (optional)
75g/3oz watercress or rocket (arugula), roughly chopped
30ml/2 tbsp crème fraîche
6 eggs, beaten
a handful of parsley, finely chopped
100g/3¾oz smoked salmon, cut into thin strips
115g/4oz/⅔ cup cooked red quinoa
50g/2oz/½ cup grated strong cheese such as Emmenthal or Parmesan
salt and ground black pepper
fresh fruit juice, to serve

1 Heat the oil in a heavy frying pan or skillet and add the onion and chopped pepper. Stir-fry for 8–10 minutes until the onion is soft, then add the garlic and fennel seeds, and cook for 2 minutes.

2 Add the watercress or rocket and cook for a few more minutes until the leaves have wilted.

3 Meanwhile, whisk together the crème fraîche, beaten egg, herbs and seasoning in a small bowl.

4 Add the salmon and quinoa to the frying pan, mix well, then spread evenly over the base of the pan.

5 Pour the beaten egg mixture into the pan, lower the heat, and cook for 5–8 minutes until the frittata is cooked most of the way through (you can test this by carefully pressing it with a fork). Covering the pan with a lid will help ensure even cooking. Heat the grill (broiler) to medium.

6 Sprinkle the grated cheese over the top of the frittata, then place under the grill, making sure the handle is not exposed to heat, for 3–5 minutes until the frittata is puffed and golden brown. Serve warm or at room temperature, with a glass of fruit juice, if you like.

Nutritional Information: Gluten Free
Energy 310kcal/1289kJ; Protein 22g; Carbohydrate 13g, of which sugars 6g; Fat 19g, of which saturates 7g; Cholesterol 237mg; Calcium 228mg; Fibre 2g; Sodium 664mg.

Substantial, rustic breads make great breakfasts, and this loaf, using cooked quinoa to add extra sustenance, is lovely when fresh from the oven for a late brunch, or toasted for a weekday breakfast. Serve sliced and buttered, or as toast, with scrambled eggs, for a breakfast that will keep you going through the most active morning.

CHEESE, ONION AND BACON BREAD

SERVES 8
225g/8oz/2 cups strong white bread flour
175g/6oz/1½ cups strong wholemeal (whole-wheat) bread flour
300g/12oz/2 cups cooked pearl quinoa
10ml/2 tsp easy blend (rapid-rise) yeast
7.5ml/1½ tsp salt
60ml/4 tbsp sugar
300ml/ ½ pint/1¼ cups lukewarm water
15ml/1 tbsp vegetable oil
1 small onion, finely diced
4 rashers (strips) streaky (fatty) bacon
50g/2oz/½ cup mature (sharp) Cheddar cheese, grated
milk, to glaze

1 Sift the flours into a large bowl, add the cooked quinoa, yeast, salt and sugar and stir to mix. Make a well in the centre and gradually mix in enough lukewarm water to form a soft dough.

2 Knead for 6–8 minutes, on a floured board, by holding the dough with one hand and stretching it with the palm of the other hand. Turn the dough and repeat this action, to stretch the dough and activate the yeast. Alternatively, knead with a dough hook in an electric mixer for 3–4 minutes.

3 Cover the bowl with a damp cloth and leave in a warm place for 1–1½ hours, until nearly doubled in size.

4 Meanwhile, in a frying pan, heat the oil and add the onion, frying for 4–5 minutes until soft but translucent.

5 Add 2 of the bacon rashers to the pan and fry for a further 3–4 minutes, until brown and crispy. Snip the cooked bacon rashers into small pieces with some kitchen scissors. Set aside.

6 When the dough has risen, knock back (punch down) and knead for a further few minutes by hand, or with an electric dough hook. Add the bacon, onion and three-quarters of the grated cheese, and fold in and knead just enough to incorporate.

7 Heat the oven to 200°C/400°F/Gas 6. Oil a 450g/1lb loaf tin (pan), or a large baking sheet if you don't have a tin. Shape the dough to neatly fill the tin, or shape into a bloomer shape if using a baking sheet. Leave to prove for another 20–30 minutes in a warm place.

8 Brush the top of the loaf with milk and bake for 15 minutes. Briefly remove from the oven and sprinkle with the remaining cheese and 2 bacon rashers. Bake for a further 15–20 minutes, until the loaf is risen and golden, then remove it from the tin. It should sound hollow on the base when tapped. Return it to the oven for a further few minutes if required.

9 Transfer the loaf to a wire rack and leave to cool. Serve sliced and buttered.

Nutritional Information:
Energy 314kcal/1325kJ; Protein 12g; Carbohydrate 51g, of which sugars 10g; Fat 8g, of which saturates 3g; Cholesterol 14mg; Calcium 103mg; Fibre 3g; Sodium 585mg.

A mixture of quinoa and spelt flour is used to make this rustic breakfast loaf. Spelt is an ancient grain (dating back more than 5,000 years), which has a lower gluten content than wheat flour. The seeds in the mixture give slow-release carbohydrates for a healthy and filling breakfast. Serve buttered with your favourite jam or marmalade.

SEEDED NUTTY SPELT BREAD

SERVES 8

225g/8oz/2 cups quinoa flour
225g/8oz/2 cups spelt flour
10ml/2 tsp easy-blend (rapid-rise) dried yeast
10ml/2 tsp salt
60ml/4 tbsp sugar
25g/1oz/¼ cup mixed seeds (sunflower, pumpkin, flax and poppy seeds), plus 15ml/1 tbsp extra, for sprinkling
25g/1oz/¼ cup roughly chopped nuts, (such as walnuts or hazelnuts)
300ml/½ pint/1¼ cups lukewarm water
oil, for greasing
milk, to glaze

1 Sift the flours into a large bowl, add the dried yeast, salt, sugar, mixed seeds and nuts, and stir to combine. Make a well in the centre.

2 Pour the lukewarm water into the well, and stir, mixing in the flour gradually, to form a pliable dough.

3 Transfer the dough to a floured board, and knead by hand for 6–8 minutes, or in an electric mixer with a dough hook.

4 To knead by hand, hold the dough with one hand and stretch it with the palm of the other hand, then folding it back. Turn the dough 90° and repeat this process for the required time.

5 Place the dough in a clean bowl, cover with a damp cloth and leave in a warm place for 1–1½ hours, until the dough has nearly doubled in size.

6 Knock back (punch down) the dough and knead for a couple of minutes. Cover with the damp cloth again and set aside to prove for another 30 minutes, until doubled in size. Preheat the oven to 220°C/425°F/Gas 7.

7 Oil a 450g/1lb loaf tin (pan), or a baking sheet. Shape the dough to neatly fill the tin, or if using the baking sheet, split it into three strands and plait (braid) it for a more decorative loaf.

8 Score the top of the loaf with a sharp knife lengthways and across, to help the dough rise. Brush the top with milk and sprinkle the top with seeds.

9 Bake for 35–40 minutes, until the loaf is risen and golden, and sounds hollow on the base when tapped (you will have to remove it from the tin to test this).

10 Remove from the tin or baking tray, and cool on a wire rack for at least 20 minutes. The bread is delicious served fresh or toasted, spread with butter and jam and accompanied by a cup of tea or coffee.

COOK'S TIP
You can use a breadmaker to make this loaf, using a basic wholegrain programme. Add the nuts and seeds to the dough halfway through the cycle, or follow the manufacturer's instructions.

Nutritional Information:
Energy 277kcal/1173kJ; Protein 21g; Carbohydrate 42g, of which sugars 8g; Fat 5g, of which saturates 2g; Cholesterol 0mg; Calcium 82mg; Fibre 3g; Sodium 3mg.

The lovely soft texture of brioche comes from the egg and milk in the dough. In this version some of the traditional 'strong' gluten-rich bread flour is substituted with some gluten-free quinoa flour to give fibre, iron and calcium. Rich and substantial, the brioche shouldn't need butter or jam, and is delicious accompanied by frothy hot chocolate.

CHOCOLATE AND APRICOT BRIOCHE

SERVES 4–6

115g/4oz/1 cup strong white bread flour
115g/4oz/1 cup quinoa flour
50g/2oz/½ cup unsweetened cocoa powder
10ml/2 tsp easy blend (rapid-rise) yeast
60ml/4 tbsp soft light brown sugar
5ml/1 tsp salt
50g/2oz/¼ cup butter, melted
3 eggs, beaten
45ml/3 tbsp milk
45ml/3 tbsp warm water
5ml/1 tsp vanilla extract
50g/2oz plain (semisweet) chocolate, chopped into chunks
50g/2oz/¼ cup dried apricots, finely chopped
30ml/2 tbsp milk and 15ml/1 tbsp soft light brown sugar, to glaze

1 Place all of the ingredients, except the chocolate and apricots, in a large bowl or in a food mixer if using a dough hook, and mix together to create a soft dough.

2 Transfer to a floured board and knead for about 10 minutes by hand, or using a dough hook in a mixer for about 5 minutes, until the dough is smooth and elastic.

3 Set aside in a bowl covered with a damp cloth and leave to rise in a warm place for about 1½ hours. It may not quite double in size, but will be soft and springy to touch.

4 Knock back (punch down) the dough and stretch it out to form a rough rectangle. Sprinkle the chocolate chunks and apricots on top and fold in the sides to envelop them. Fold and knead again until the chocolate and apricots are evenly distributed through the dough.

5 Re-mould the dough into two manageable balls and then shape as desired; you can divide it into 12 smaller brioche rolls, plait (braid) it or form it into a more traditional round shape. Leave it to prove for 30 minutes until risen again. Preheat the oven to 190°C/375°F/Gas 5.

6 When ready, place the shaped dough on to a greased baking tray, brush with the milk and sprinkle with soft light brown sugar.

7 Bake in the centre of the oven until the brioche has a crispy top and sounds hollow when tapped on the bottom. This will take about 30 minutes for a larger loaf, but only 10–15 minutes for smaller brioche rolls.

COOK'S TIP

Kneading well and proving in a warm place will help this lower-gluten loaf to stretch and rise. If time is tight, you can omit the second prove at step 3; the loaf will just have a slightly closer texture.

Nutritional Information:
Energy 335kcal/1410kJ; Protein 9g; Carbohydrate 46g, of which sugars 18g; Fat 14g, of which saturates 8g; Cholesterol 82mg; Calcium 105mg; Fibre 2g; Sodium 471mg.

The combination of sugar and cinnamon is perfect at breakfast, especially with a cup of aromatic coffee. Fresh bread provides a great opportunity to get children involved in kneading and shaping. You can prepare these rolls the night before, keeping the shaped, uncooked dough in the refrigerator overnight for baking the next morning.

OAT AND CINNAMON BREAKFAST ROLLS

MAKES 12

350g/12oz/3 cups strong white bread flour
115g/4oz/1 cup quinoa flakes
50g/2oz/scant 1/2 cup rolled oats
10ml/2 tsp easy blend (rapid-rise) dried yeast
7.5ml/1 1/2 tsp salt
30ml/2 tbsp soft light brown sugar
10ml/2 tsp ground cinnamon
175ml/6fl oz/3/4 cup boiled water
175ml/6fl oz/3/4 cup milk
a little milk and 10ml/2 tsp soft light brown sugar, to glaze
butter and clear honey or fresh fruit, to serve

1 Sift the flour into a large bowl, then stir in the quinoa flakes, oats and dried yeast. Make a well in the centre.

2 Mix the boiled water with the milk to make a lukewarm liquid, then add this to the dry ingredients, stirring to form a pliable dough.

3 Transfer the dough to a floured board and knead for 5–8 minutes by holding the dough with one hand and stretching it with the palm of the other hand. Turn the dough and repeat this action until the dough is smooth and elastic. Alternatively, knead with a dough hook in an electric mixer for 3–4 minutes.

4 Place the dough in a lightly oiled bowl, cover with a damp cloth and leave in a warm place for 1–1 1/2 hours, until nearly doubled in size.

5 Knock back (punch down) the dough and knead for a further few minutes by hand, or with an electric dough hook.

6 Divide the dough into 12 rolls, plaiting (braiding) or shaping them as desired. Place on greased baking sheets.

7 Glaze the rolls with milk, sprinkle with light brown sugar and leave to prove for a further 20 minutes in a warm place. Preheat the oven to 220°C/425°F/Gas 7. Or, if you want to cook them fresh for breakfast the next morning, place the trays in the refrigerator at this point.

8 Bake for 12–15 minutes, until the rolls are risen and golden and sound hollow when tapped. Allow to cool on a wire rack for 15 minutes. They are delicious served warm with clear honey and a platter of fresh fruit. If cooking the next morning, remove from the refrigerator and bring to room temperature while the oven heats.

COOK'S TIP
You can use a breadmaker on a basic wholegrain programme to make these.

VARIATION
Add a mashed banana and 30ml/2 tbsp finely chopped walnuts with the liquid to make Banana and Walnut Rolls.

Nutritional Information, per 2 rolls:
Energy 330kcal/1397kJ; Protein 12g; Carbohydrate 65g, of which sugars 8g; Fat 4g, of which saturates 1g; Cholesterol 4mg; Calcium 162mg; Fibre 2g; Sodium 462mg.

Quinoa flour takes the place of ordinary flour to make a healthier pancake. You can serve these lovely crêpes with many different toppings: sugar and lemon is traditional, but you could also offer jam, honey, or chocolate spread for people to choose from. Here they are filled with strawberries and creamy yogurt for a great start to the day.

QUINOA CRÊPES

MAKES 8
115g/4oz/1 cup quinoa flour
1 large (US extra large) egg
350ml/12fl oz/1½ cups milk
30ml/2 tbsp vegetable oil, for frying
strawberries, sliced, and Greek (US strained plain) yogurt, to serve

1 Sift the flour into a large bowl and make a well in the centre. Beat the egg and milk together in a jug (pitcher). Pour the egg mixture into the flour well, and use a whisk to slowly incorporate the flour mixture, a little at a time, to make a smooth batter.

2 Alternatively place all of the ingredients into a bowl or liquidizer, and blend with a hand blender or food processor until smooth.

3 Heat a little oil in a frying pan until it is hot but not smoking. Add enough batter to cover the base of the pan, tipping it quickly to ensure that it spreads evenly.

4 Cook over medium heat until the pancake is set and golden underneath, then flip it using a spatula. Cook the other side for a couple of minutes, until golden brown.

5 Add a little more oil to the pan and repeat until all the batter has been used, keeping the cooked pancakes warm in a low oven until ready for serving. Make sure your pan is well oiled before cooking each pancake.

6 Serve the pancakes warm, filled with strawberries and yogurt, or whichever selection of fillings you prefer.

VARIATION
For a substantial savoury option, fill cooked pancakes with a rasher (strip) of grilled (broiled) bacon, grilled tomato slices and black pepper.

Nutritional Information per 2 pancakes: Gluten free Energy 226kcal/946kJ; Protein 7g; Carbohydrate 23g, of which sugars 4g; Fat 13g, of which saturates 5g; Cholesterol 56mg; Calcium 128mg; Fibre 1g; Sodium 52mg.

Making pancakes is a lovely sociable way to start the weekend, when all the family can get involved in making them. Those tucking in won't notice any difference between these and regular pancakes, happily oblivious to the nutritional boost that quinoa gives them, with its slow-release energy and micronutrients.

LEMON AND RAISIN PANCAKES

MAKES 16

1 egg
120ml/4fl oz/ ½ cup plain yogurt
120ml/4fl oz/ ½ cup milk
115g/4oz/1 cup quinoa flour
15ml/1 tbsp baking powder
50g/2oz/ ¼ cup sugar
grated rind of 1 lemon
25g/1oz/ ⅕ cup raisins
vegetable oil, for frying
butter and maple syrup, to serve

1 Whisk the egg, yogurt and milk in a jug (pitcher) until combined. Put the flour and baking powder into a large bowl and make a well in the middle.

2 Add the egg mixture to the well and use a whisk to incorporate the flour mixture, a little at a time, to make a smooth batter. Add the sugar and lemon rind. Allow to stand for 20 minutes.

3 When you are ready to cook, pour a little oil into a frying pan or pancake pan and use kitchen paper to spread it evenly over the base.

4 Place the pan over medium heat, and when hot spoon in enough batter to form two or three pancakes, about 6–7.5cm/ 2½–3in in diameter.

5 Sprinkle a few raisins on each pancake and cook for 1–2 minutes on each side.

6 When the pancakes are puffed and bubbly, and golden on both sides, remove from the pan, top with a knob of butter, and keep warm while you cook the remaining batter. Serve the pancakes warm with extra butter, if you wish, and maple syrup poured over.

VARIATIONS
• Use fresh blueberries instead of raisins, if you wish.
• Try serving the pancakes with some crispy grilled (broiled) bacon for a traditional American breakfast.

Nutritional Information: Gluten free
Energy 258kcal/1088kJ; Protein 6g; Carbohydrate 42g, of which sugars 20g; Fat 9g, of which saturates 3g; Cholesterol 34mg; Calcium 99mg; Fibre 2g; Sodium 45mg.

Eating breakfast means you won't be tempted to buy high-calorie, high-fat snacks midmorning. If you feel you don't have time for breakfast on weekdays before rushing out of the house, take a portable powershake and breakfast bar with you. Together, these give you a healthy, low-glycaemic, high-calcium and protein-rich start to the day.

BREAKFAST BARS WITH QUINOA POWERSHAKE

APPLE AND GINGER BREAKFAST BARS

MAKES 8
150ml/ ¼ pint/ ⅔ cup clear honey
40g/1½oz/3 tbsp butter
45ml/3 tbsp demerara (raw) sugar
2 small or 1 large eating apple, peeled
and grated
30ml/2 tbsp puffed quinoa
30ml/2 tbsp ground flaxseeds (linseeds)
30ml/2 tbsp roughly chopped hazelnuts
2.5ml/ ½ tsp ground cloves
5ml/1 tsp mixed (apple pie) spice
10ml/2 tsp ground ginger

1 Heat the oven to 180°C/350°F/Gas 4. Grease a 18cm/7in square baking tin (pan), and line with baking parchment.

2 In a large pan over low heat, heat the honey, butter and sugar, stirring, until the sugar has dissolved, and you have a thin syrup.

3 Remove the pan from the heat and stir in the remaining ingredients, until thoroughly combined. Transfer to the prepared tin and spread evenly into the edges with the back of a fork.

COOK'S TIP
Puffed quinoa is available in health food stores or online. If you can't get hold of it, use twice the weight of quinoa flakes.

4 Bake for 30–35 minutes until crisp at the edges. Score into eight bars with a sharp knife while still warm, but leave in the tin until totally cool. Wrap each one in clear film (plastic wrap) and store in an airtight container.

Nutritional Information: Gluten Free
Energy 174kcal/731kJ; Protein 2g; Carbohydrate 26g, of which sugars 22g; Fat 8g, of which saturates 2g; Cholesterol 10mg; Calcium 16mg; Fibre 1g; Sodium 35mg.

QUINOA POWERSHAKE

SERVES 1
1 small banana, peeled and sliced
200ml/7fl oz/scant 1 cup milk
115g/4oz/ ½ cup Greek (US strained
plain) yogurt
30ml/2 tbsp quinoa flakes
5ml/1 tsp honey
a pinch each of ground nutmeg and
cinnamon

1 Blend all of the ingredients in a blender or food processor until smooth.

2 Pour into a glass and drink immediately, or transfer into a portable vessel and take it with you for a breakfast on the move.

Nutritional Information: Gluten free
Energy 491kcal/2050kJ; Protein 18g; Carbohydrate 56g, of which sugars 37g; Fat 21g, of which saturates 13g; Cholesterol 47mg; Calcium 419mg; Fibre 5g; Sodium 170mg.

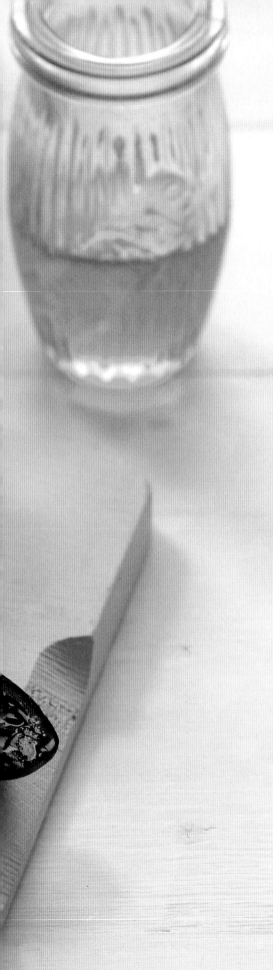

APPETIZERS AND SALADS

Quinoa is a superb salad ingredient, as
it can carry a range of full flavours and
robust ingredients, and when mixed
with raw vegetables results in dishes
that are packed with nutrients. Quinoa
can also add bulk to soups, and it
makes great falafel, pastry treats
and dips for tempting snacks
and appetizers.

This lovely spicy soup is brimming with nutrients: heart-healthy antioxidants like lycopene and beta carotene, and vitamin C, together with low-GI lentils and quinoa. Harissa is a hot, deeply flavoured African paste made from red pepper, chilli, garlic, paprika, coriander, cumin and rose petals. It packs a punch, so use less of it if you wish.

FRESH TOMATO AND BLACK QUINOA SOUP

SERVES 4
30ml/2 tbsp vegetable oil
1 medium onion, roughly chopped
3 cloves garlic, crushed
10ml/2 tsp harissa (chilli sauce)
12 plum tomatoes (about 675g/1½lb),
    roughly chopped
175g/6oz/1 cup black quinoa
175g/6oz/¾ cup red lentils
30ml/2 tbsp sun-dried tomatoes,
    roughly chopped
1.75 litres/3 pints/7½ cups vegetable
    stock
salt and ground black pepper

To serve
5ml/1 tsp harissa
30ml/2 tbsp natural (plain) yogurt
1 sun-dried tomato, finely chopped
warmed crusty bread

1 Heat the oil in a large pan, then add the chopped onion and garlic. Cook for 2–3 minutes on a medium heat, stirring, until softened.

2 Stir the harissa into the onions, then add the chopped tomatoes and cook for a further 5 minutes on a lower heat to release the aromatic flavours from the harissa into the vegetables.

3 Add the quinoa, lentils, sun-dried tomatoes and stock, then bring to the boil. Lower the heat, cover, and simmer for 12–14 minutes, until the quinoa is soft to bite and the lentils are tender. Season to taste with salt and pepper and add a little more harissa if you wish.

4 In a small bowl, swirl together, but don't completely mix, the yogurt and harissa for serving.

5 Pour the soup into four warmed bowls and top with a spoonful of the harissa yogurt. Sprinkle a few chopped sun-dried tomatoes on top and serve with warmed crusty bread.

COOK'S TIP
Add more water to the soup at the end of step 3, and blend in a liquidizer if you prefer a thinner, smoother soup.

Nutritional Information: Gluten free with GF free stock
Energy 257kcal/1084kJ; Protein 11g; Carbohydrate 41g, of which sugars 12g; Fat 7g, of which saturates 1g; Cholesterol 0mg; Calcium 150mg; Fibre 6g; Sodium 583mg.

Red quinoa adds striking colour and texture to this rich and sustaining rustic soup. Most of the ingredients are everyday standbys, meaning that you can easily make it when a quick lunch is needed, substituting fresh kale for frozen or tinned vegetables if necessary. This soup is lovely served with slices of warm Bacon, Cheese and Onion Bread.

TUSCAN BEAN SOUP

SERVES 4
15ml/1 tbsp vegetable oil
1 medium onion, finely diced
2 cloves garlic, peeled and crushed
75g/3oz curly kale, finely sliced
115g/4oz/^{2}/$_3$ cup red quinoa, rinsed
250g/8oz/1½ cups canned red kidney
   beans
400g/14oz can chopped tomatoes
1.2 litres/2 pints/5 cups vegetable stock
10ml/2 tsp mixed dried herbs
30ml/2 tbsp tomato purée (paste)
30ml/2 tbsp balsamic vinegar
handful of fresh basil leaves, torn
salt and ground black pepper
crème fraîche and fresh bread,
   to serve

1 Heat the oil in a large pan, add the onion, garlic and kale and fry on a medium heat for 4 minutes, until the onion is soft.

2 Add the red quinoa, kidney beans, chopped tomatoes, stock, dried herbs, tomato purée and balsamic vinegar and bring to the boil.

3 Reduce the heat and simmer gently for about 15 minutes, until the quinoa is tender to bite.

4 Remove from the heat and add the basil, reserving a few leaves for garnishing, and season as required.

5 Divide into four bowls and top each with a spoonful of crème fraîche and a couple of basil leaves. Serve with fresh, warm bread.

COOK'S TIP
If not serving immediately, you may need to add another cupful of stock or water when reheating.

VARIATIONS
• Swap fresh kale for the same weight of frozen peas or spinach, if fresh supplies are limited.
• Add 10ml/2 tsp harissa paste for a spicy soup.

Nutritional Information: Gluten free with GF stock
Energy 257kcal/1084kJ; Protein 11g; Carbohydrate 41g, of which sugars 12g; Fat 7g, of which saturates 1g; Cholesterol 0mg: Calcium 150mg; Fibre 6g; Sodium 583mg.

This fresh-tasting, nutritious soup will warm your core and tantalize your tastebuds on a chilly day. The combination of fresh and preserved lemons, often used in Moroccan cuisine, makes for a sharp, zesty stock that stimulates the senses. Black quinoa complements the vibrant colours of carrot and parsley, but pearl quinoa would work well too.

LEMON CHICKEN SOUP

SERVES 4
30ml/2 tbsp olive oil
1 medium onion, finely chopped
115g/4oz/1½ cups chopped
    mushrooms,
2 carrots, peeled and finely diced
150g/5oz/scant 1 cup black quinoa
1 litre/1¾ pints/4 cups chicken stock
2 skinned chicken breast fillets, about
    250g/9oz total weight, sliced in
    1cm/ ½in strips
juice, and grated rind, of 1 lemon
1 preserved lemon, finely chopped
a good handful of chopped parsley,
    finely chopped
salt and ground black pepper
crusty bread, to serve

1 Heat the oil in a deep pan, add the onion and soften for 2–3 minutes, stirring all the time.

2 Turn up the heat, add the mushrooms and fry for another 2–3 minutes, until the liquid is released, then evaporates.

3 Add the diced carrots, quinoa and stock to the pan and bring to the boil.

4 Add the chicken strips, lemon juice and rind and preserved lemon to the pan. Bring back to the boil, then cover, reduce the heat and simmer for around 12–14 minutes, until the quinoa is cooked but still al dente.

5 Remove from the heat, stir in the chopped parsley, and season to taste with salt and pepper.

6 Pour the soup into warmed bowls, and serve with bread.

COOK'S TIP
Black quinoa has a slightly firmer texture than pearl quinoa once cooked.

VARIATION
Substitute the chicken with a can of borlotti beans for a vegetarian alternative, or stir in some tofu cubes just before serving.

Nutritional Information: Gluten free with GF stock
Energy 313kcal/1307kJ; Protein 26g; Carbohydrate 27g, of which sugars 5g; Fat 11g, of which saturates 2g; Cholesterol 58mg; Calcium 79mg; Fibre 4g; Sodium 56mg.

Cooked quinoa blends beautifully in this deeply flavoured Spanish-style dip, which with its abundant tomatoes and wonderful fresh basil will bring back happy memories of summer sun. Quick and very easy to make, this dip is ideal served with tasty pastry twists, made with quinoa flour, for pre-dinner snacks or picnics.

MANCHEGO AND SUN-DRIED TOMATO DIP WITH QUINOA POPPY TWISTS

SERVES 4

For the poppy twists
175g/6oz/1½ cups quinoa flour
50g/2oz/½ cup plain (all-purpose) flour
60ml/4 tbsp cup poppy seeds
10ml/2 tsp mixed dried herbs
2.5ml/½ tsp salt
75ml/2½fl oz/⅓ cup olive oil
150ml/¼ pint/⅔ cup cold water
ground black pepper, to taste
milk, to glaze

For the dip
75g/3oz/scant ½ cup cream cheese
30ml/2 tbsp grated Manchego cheese
30ml/2 tbsp sun-dried tomatoes, roughly chopped
45ml/3 tbsp passata (bottled strained tomatoes)
75g/3oz/½ cup cooked quinoa
a good handful of fresh thyme leaves, roughly chopped, plus some left whole to garnish
salt and ground black pepper
15ml/1 tbsp virgin olive oil, if needed

1 Preheat the oven to 190°C/ 375°F/ Gas 5. Line a medium baking sheet with baking parchment.

2 To make the poppy twists, sift the flours together in a large bowl. Mix in the poppy seeds, herbs and seasoning. Stir in the oil, and then the cold water little by little to form a soft, pliable pastry.

3 Shape into a disc, wrap in clear film (plastic wrap) and chill for 30 minutes in the refrigerator.

4 Make the dip using a food processor or blender. Process the cream cheese, Manchego cheese, sun-dried tomatoes, passata, cooked quinoa and chopped thyme until smooth. Season to taste and mix in the oil, a little at a time, to loosen, if needed. Transfer to a serving bowl, cover and chill.

5 On a floured board, roll the pastry into a rough rectangle about 6 x 12cm/2½ x 4½in and 1cm/½in thick.

6 Cut the pastry into 12 even strips, then twist each one a couple of times as you transfer them to the prepared baking sheet.

7 Brush the twists with milk and bake for 15–18 minutes, until golden-brown and crisp. Transfer to a wire rack to cool.

8 Garnish the dip with thyme leaves and a good sprinkling of black pepper, and serve with the poppy twists

VARIATION
For the twists you could use wholemeal (whole-wheat) flour instead of white flour, if you wish, and add 30ml/2 tbsp finely chopped olives to the pastry mix.

Twists Nutritional Information (3 twists):
Energy 364kcal/1524kJ; Protein 9g; Carbohydrate 41g, of which sugars 0g; Fat 28g, of which saturates 6g; Cholesterol 0mg; Calcium 231mg; Fibre 2g; Sodium 308mg.

Dip Nutritional Information: Gluten free
Energy 185kcal/767kJ; Protein 4g; Carbohydrate 7g, of which sugars 3g; Fat 16g, of which saturates 8g; Cholesterol 24mg; Calcium 99mg; Fibre 1g; Sodium 142mg.

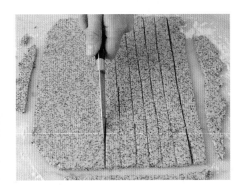

This delightful, creamy dip, served with crispy Parmesan pastry straws, would make a perfect beginning to a drinks party or summer barbecue. Edamame beans are young soya beans and are usually sold frozen. They are a rich source of isoflavines, so when they are teamed up with quinoa they create an appetizer that is full of protein.

EDAMAME BEAN DIP WITH PARMESAN STRAWS

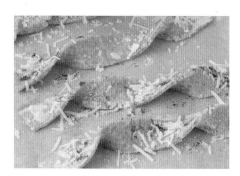

SERVES 4

For the Parmesan straws
75g/3oz/²/₃ cup wholemeal (whole-wheat) flour
75g/3oz/³/₄ cup quinoa flakes
75g/3oz/1 cup grated Parmesan cheese, plus extra for sprinkling
75g/3oz/6 tbsp butter, softened
cold water, to bind
milk, for glazing
paprika, for sprinkling

For the edamame bean and chive dip
75g/3oz/¹/₂ cup frozen edamame beans, cooked
50g/2oz/¹/₃ cup pearl quinoa, cooked
60ml/4 tbsp sour cream
60ml/4 tbsp mayonnaise
30ml/2 tbsp fresh chives, chopped, plus extra for garnishing
15ml/1 tbsp fresh coriander (cilantro), roughly chopped
salt and ground black pepper
paprika, for sprinkling

1 For the Parmesan straws, place the flour and quinoa flakes in a large bowl and mix with the grated Parmesan.

2 Add the butter and, using your fingertips, rub in the fat until the mixture resembles fine breadcrumbs. Add just enough water to bind everything into a firm dough.

3 Wrap the dough in clear film (plastic wrap) and chill in the refrigerator for 30 minutes. Heat the oven to 180°C/350°F/Gas 4.

4 Line a baking tray with baking parchment. On a floured board, roll the pastry into a rectangle shape and score into 'straw' shapes, about 2 x 5cm/³/₄ x 2in.

5 Brush the pastry straws with milk, then sprinkle with grated Parmesan and a little paprika.

6 Press the cheese gently with your fingertips to help it adhere to the pastry, then carefully transfer the straws to the baking tray. Bake for 10–12 minutes, until golden and crisp. Transfer to a wire rack to cool.

7 Meanwhile, prepare the dip by blending all the ingredients in a food processor until smooth and creamy.

8 Transfer to a bowl, sprinkle with chives and a little paprika, and serve with the warm Parmesan straws.

VARIATION
Substitute edamame beans for other canned beans, such as cannellini. You could also use an equivalent amount of podded and peeled fresh, young broad (fava) beans.

Straws Nutritional Information per 4 straws:
Energy 344kcal/1433kJ; Protein 12g; Carbohydrate 24g, of which sugars 1g; Fat 23g, of which saturates 14g; Cholesterol 57mg; Calcium 225mg; Fibre 2g; Sodium 260mg.

Dip Nutritional Information: Gluten free with GF mayonnaise. Energy 169kcal/700kJ; Protein 4g; Carbohydrate 4g, of which sugars 1g; Fat 15g, of which saturates; 40g; Cholesterol 20mg; Calcium 37mg; Fibre 1g; Sodium 72mg.

Falafel originated in Egypt and evolved as street food in the Middle East, served with salad and tahini in pitta bread, or served as part of a mezze. They are most often made with broad beans, or chickpeas, but here quinoa makes a tasty and effective addition. The crunchy slaw and herby dressing complement the spicy falafel perfectly.

QUINOA FALAFEL WITH RED CABBAGE SLAW

SERVES 4

For the falafel
250g/9oz/1 cup canned chickpeas
   (drained weight)
225g/8oz/1½ cups cooked pearl quinoa
25g/1oz/¼ cup quinoa flour
1 medium onion, finely diced
a good handful of fresh coriander
   (cilantro), finely chopped
4 cloves garlic, crushed
30ml/2 tbsp crème fraîche
10ml/2 tsp ground cumin
10ml/2 tsp ground coriander
15ml/1 tbsp Tabasco sauce
45ml/3 tbsp quinoa flour, for shaping
45ml/3 tbsp rapeseed (canola) oil
salt and ground black pepper, to taste
4 warmed pitta breads, sliced up the
   edge, to serve

For the dressing
150g/5oz/scant ⅔ cup natural
   (plain) yogurt
5ml/1 tsp ground coriander
1 clove garlic, crushed
5ml/1 tsp tomato purée (paste)
5ml/1 tsp fresh coriander (cilantro),
   finely chopped

For the red cabbage slaw
50g/2oz/⅓ cup very finely sliced
   red cabbage
50g/2oz/⅓ cup peeled and
   grated carrot
2 spring onions (scallions), finely sliced
60ml/4 tbsp crème fraîche

1 First make the falafel mixture. Place the chickpeas, cooked pearl quinoa, quinoa flour, onion, coriander, garlic, crème fraîche, cumin, ground coriander and Tabasco sauce in a food processor.

2 Season well with salt and pepper and gradually pulse until the mixture is blended, but not completely smooth.

3 If preparing by hand, in a large bowl, break up the chickpeas using the flat end of the rolling pin, then beat them into the rest of the ingredients.

4 Using your hands, roll the mixture into 16 balls, using quinoa flour to prevent the mixture sticking. You can set these aside in the refrigerator at this stage if you like, for cooking later.

5 Prepare the yogurt dressing by mixing together the ingredients in a small bowl. Season to taste and chill.

6 Prepare the cabbage slaw by mixing together all of the ingredients in a bowl, season to taste and chill.

7 Heat the rapeseed oil in a large frying pan and lightly fry the falafels for about 5–8 minutes, turning regularly to ensure even browning. Fry in batches if the frying pan isn't large enough to hold all of them. Drain the falafel on kitchen paper, until they are all cooked.

8 Serve warm, or at room temperature, tucked into a pitta bread, filled with cabbage slaw and drizzled with coriander and yogurt dressing.

VARIATION
Falafel are also great cold, dipped in hummus, as part of a picnic.

Nutritional Information: Gluten free without pitta
Energy 621kcal/2609kJ; Protein 20g; Carbohydrate 84g, of which sugars 11g; Fat 26g, of which saturates 8g; Cholesterol 25mg; Calcium 280mg; Fibre 6g; Sodium 596mg.

These crisp little pastry packages make a great appetizer, served with mint jelly. They are also good lunch box fillers. Red quinoa adds colour to the filling, but white quinoa would work perfectly well. If time is tight, use store-bought filo pastry instead of making your own, although you won't benefit from the double quinoa hit.

COURGETTE, FETA AND MINT QUINOA PASTIES

SERVES 4

For the pastry
75g/3oz/6 tbsp butter, softened
275g/10oz/2½ cups quinoa flour
10ml/2 tsp Dijon mustard
175ml/6fl oz/¾ cup cold water
milk, for brushing
mint jelly, to serve

For the filling
1 medium courgette (zucchini)
1 cooking apple, about 115g/4oz in
    weight, peeled, cored and grated
275g/10oz/1⅔ cups cooked red quinoa
300g/11oz feta cheese, crumbled
15ml/1 tbsp fresh mint, torn
ground black pepper

1 Make the pastry. Rub the butter into the flour in a large bowl, until the mixture resembles fine breadcrumbs.

2 Add the mustard to the bowl, and then gradually add enough cold water to make a smooth dough. Wrap in clear film (plastic wrap) and chill in the refrigerator for 30 minutes.

3 Grate the courgette straight on to a dish towel or several pieces of kitchen paper. Roll up the towel or paper and squeeze over a sink or bowl to remove excess water.

4 Transfer the grated and squeezed courgette to a large bowl and add the grated apple. Mix in the crumbled feta cheese, mint and black pepper. Preheat the oven to 190°C/375°F/Gas 5.

5 Divide the chilled pastry into two pieces, roll out and cut each into four circles about 13cm/5in in diameter.

6 Divide the filling between the eight pastry rounds, positioning it on one half of each circle.

7 Fold over the other half of the circle to enclose the filling, and press the edges together to make a small pasty shape. Crimp the edges for decorative effect and make a small slit in the top of each one.

8 Place the pasties on baking sheets (no oiling needed) and brush the tops with a little milk. Bake for 20–25 minutes, until the pastry is crisp and golden. Serve warm with mint jelly.

COOK'S TIP
Make mini pasties, if you wish, for appetizers to hand round with drinks. Reduce the cooking time slightly to about 15 minutes, depending on how small they are. Keep an eye on them and remove from the oven once they are golden-brown.

VARIATION
For Cheese and Onion Pasties, replace the grated apple with finely chopped onion, and the feta cheese with mature (sharp) Cheddar cheese.

Nutritional Information: Gluten free
Energy 618kcal/2585kJ; Protein 22g; Carbohydrate 63g, of which sugars 5g; Fat 33g, of which saturates 22g; Cholesterol 85mg; Calcium 339mg; Fibre 6g; Sodium 1134mg.

Sprouted quinoa, like any sprouted seeds, is highly nutritious, as your body gets the benefit of new little raw shoots that have lost nothing through cooking or storage. This tasty salad is crisp, raw and colourful, containing a good range of antioxidants as well as being a treat for both your body and your senses.

SPROUTED QUINOA ORIENTAL NUT SALAD

SERVES 4
75g/3oz broccoli, cut into bitesize florets
half of 1 yellow and half of 1 red (bell) pepper, cut into thin strips
50g/2oz/ 1/2 cup cashew nuts
15ml/1 tbsp sesame oil
1 1/2 cups quinoa sprouts (from about 75g/3oz/ 1/2 cup quinoa – see below)
115g/4oz/ 1/2 cup beansprouts (that can be eaten raw)
50g/2oz/scant 1/2 cup grated carrot

For the oriental dressing
15ml/1 tbsp toasted sesame oil
15ml/1 tbsp mirin
15ml/1 tbsp soy sauce
ground black pepper

1 In a small pan of boiling water, lightly steam the broccoli florets for around 2–3 minutes until softened but still slightly crisp to bite.

2 Toss the pepper and nuts with the sesame oil on an ovenproof tray. Place under a medium grill (broiler) for 5–6 minutes, until the nuts are brown and the peppers softened. Roughly crush the nuts with the end of a rolling pin.

3 Place the quinoa sprouts, beansprouts and grated carrot in a medium bowl, then add the steamed broccoli, nuts and peppers.

4 Make the dressing by shaking the ingredients together in a closed container, or whisking in a bowl.

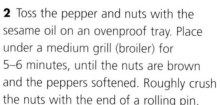

5 To serve, pour the dressing over the salad, toss and divide between four dishes. Serve as a side salad with grilled (broiled) meat or fish, or as a light meal topped with prawns (shrimp) or marinated tofu.

VARIATIONS
• Using toasted sesame seed oil adds to the depth of flavour, but regular sesame or vegetable oil will be fine too.
• Serve as a stir-fry. Before adding the dressing in step 4, stir-fry the ingredients in 15ml/1 tbsp vegetable oil, pour over the oriental marinade and serve.

GROWING QUINOA SPROUTS
Quinoa sprouts grow to about three times the seeds' original volume and need a day or two to get to a reasonable size. Rinse the quinoa in a sieve (strainer), using your fingers to remove the natural saponin coating.
 Cover in 2cm/1in water and leave for an hour. Thoroughly drain off the excess water, shaking well, and place the sprouts in a thin layer in a shallow dish. Cover with a dish towel and place in a cool, dark place for 10–12 hours.
 Repeat the rinsing, spreading and covering process two or three times to grow longer sprouts. Once prepared, the sprouts will keep for up to 3 days in a refrigerator, but the longer ones will spoil sooner.

....
Nutritional Information: Gluten free with GF soy sauce
Energy 203kcal/848kJ; Protein 7g; Carbohydrate 21g, of which sugars 7g; Fat 11g, of which saturates 2g; Cholesterol 0mg; Calcium 41mg; Fibre 2g; Sodium 269mg.

A mixture of shiitake and dried porcini mushrooms in this salad provides a rich, almost meaty flavour that gives neutral quinoa the taste boost that it needs. The result is a substantial salad with vibrant colours, an opulent sesame taste and a very useful profile of vitamins, antioxidants, iron and calcium.

SHIITAKE MUSHROOM AND SESAME SALAD

SERVES 4
12g/½oz dried porcini mushrooms
175g/6oz/1 cup tricolour quinoa
475ml/16fl oz/2 cups water
15ml/1 tbsp sesame oil
1 clove garlic, crushed
2cm/1in piece fresh root ginger, peeled and finely chopped
1 red and 1 orange (bell) pepper, sliced in thin strips
115g/4oz shiitake mushrooms, roughly torn
30ml/2 tbsp sesame seeds
salt and ground black pepper

For the dressing
5ml/1 tsp toasted sesame oil
15ml/1 tbsp rice vinegar
2.5ml/½ tsp Dijon mustard

To serve
1 small Little Gem (Bibb) lettuce, leaves separated
¼ cucumber, sliced into thin strips

1 Bring the porcini mushrooms, quinoa and water to the boil in a medium pan, lower the heat and simmer for 12–14 minutes. Drain, discarding any excess water, and set aside to cool.

2 In another pan, heat the sesame oil, add the garlic, ginger and peppers and stir-fry until the peppers are softened.

3 Add the shiitake mushrooms and cook for a further 3–4 minutes, until the mushrooms are lightly browned.

4 Dry roast the sesame seeds in a frying pan for 2–3 minutes, until they are just browned and fragrant, regularly turning to prevent them from burning.

5 In a large bowl, mix together the cooked quinoa and porcini mushrooms, the pepper and mushroom mixture and the toasted seeds. Leave to cool.

6 Make the dressing by shaking the ingredients together in a sealed container, or whisking in a small bowl.

7 Pour the dressing over the cooled salad. Serve in bowls lined with lettuce leaves accompanied by wedges of crisp, salted cucumber.

VARIATION
To serve the salad warm, add the dressing to the warm quinoa and vegetables after step 3 and serve with meaty sausages, if you like.

COOK'S TIP
Tricolour quinoa, a mixture of red, black and white grains, is widely available, but you can also make up the mix yourself.

....
Nutritional Information: Gluten free
Energy 287kcal/1203kJ; Protein 10g; Carbohydrate 36g, of which sugars 8g; Fat 13g, of which saturates 2g; Cholesterol 0mg; Calcium 113mg; Fibre 6g; Sodium 51mg.

This is a quinoa-rich variation of the classic Italian salad. The unmistakable flavours and smells of ripe tomatoes instantly recalls the Mediterranean climate. Good-quality sun-dried tomatoes are restored to plumpness after soaking. Complemented by fresh tomatoes, this is a perfect salad for al fresco dining on summer nights.

TRICOLORE QUINOA SALAD

SERVES 4
45ml/3 tbsp pine nuts
75g/3oz/ ½ cup pearl quinoa
50g/2oz sun-dried tomatoes, rehydrated in boiling water for 2 hours
25g/1oz fresh basil leaves
225g/8oz fresh mozzarella cheese, chopped or torn into small pieces
about 20 cherry tomatoes, or 8 ripe plum tomatoes, cut in half
salt and ground black pepper
cured Italian meats and ciabatta bread, to serve

For the dressing
90ml/6 tbsp balsamic vinegar
45ml/3 tbsp olive oil
2.5ml/ ½ tsp Dijon mustard
1 garlic clove, crushed
salt and ground black pepper

1 Dry-fry the pine nuts in a heavy frying pan, stirring all the time, for about 4–5 minutes until lightly browned. Be careful the pine nuts don't scorch. Set aside to cool.

2 Cook the quinoa in 250ml/8fl oz/ 1 cup water for 15–17 minutes, until tender, but retaining some bite. Drain and set aside to cool.

3 Drain the sun-dried tomatoes, pat dry with kitchen paper, and cut with a sharp knife into long, thin strips.

4 Tear or snip one quarter of the basil leaves into pieces and place in a jar or small bowl. Add all the dressing ingredients and shake or whisk to mix.

5 Place the cooled quinoa, pine nuts, mozzarella, sun-dried tomatoes and cherry tomatoes in a bowl. Tear the remaining basil leaves, add to the bowl, pour in the dressing, and toss gently to mix. Check the seasoning, adding more salt and pepper if needed.

6 Serve alongside a cold platter of meats, accompanied by fresh ciabatta.

Nutritional Information: Gluten free
Energy 447kcal/1864kJ; Protein 16g; Carbohydrate 27g, of which sugars 14g; Fat 31g, of which saturates 10g; Cholesterol 32mg; Calcium 234mg; Fibre 3g; Sodium 303mg.

Wholegrains such as quinoa and buckwheat are absorbed more slowly than refined grains, so they keep you satisfied for longer. They may also help fight diabetes and obesity. They are easy to prepare, and tasty when combined with other grains such as pearled spelt and wheatberries. Toasting gives a richness and greater depth of flavour.

TOASTED GRAIN, FENNEL AND ORANGE SALAD

SERVES 4
75g/3oz/ 1/3 cup wheatberries
175ml/6fl oz/ 3/4 cup boiling water
75g/3oz/ 1/2 cup pearled spelt
75g/3oz/ 1/2 cup buckwheat
115g/4oz/ 2/3 cup red quinoa, rinsed
750ml/1 1/4 pints/3 cups vegetable stock
50g/2oz/ 1/2 cup blanched whole
  almonds, cut in half
1 fennel bulb, outer leaves removed,
  finely sliced
1 orange, peeled and segmented,
  all white pith removed
a good handful of parsley,
  finely chopped
rocket (arugula) or lettuce leaves,
  to serve

For the dressing
60ml/4 tbsp olive oil
30ml/2 tbsp cider vinegar
5ml/1 tsp wholegrain mustard
ground black pepper

1 Place the wheatberries in a small pan and dry-fry for 4–6 minutes, until lightly browned. Add the boiling water, being careful as it hits the hot pan, and simmer for 35–40 minutes until the wheatberries are tender to bite. Drain, discarding any excess water.

2 Meanwhile, in large pan, dry-fry the spelt, buckwheat and quinoa for 4–6 minutes, stirring, until lightly browned. Add the vegetable stock to the pan and simmer for 20–25 minutes, until the grains are tender to bite.

3 Meanwhile, toast the almonds under a medium grill (broiler) for 6–8 minutes, until lightly browned. Watch them all the time as it is easy to scorch them.

4 Make the dressing by shaking the ingredients together in a jar, or whisking together in a small bowl.

5 Mix the cooked wheatberries with the other warm grains in a large bowl. Add the toasted almonds along with the fennel, orange and parsley. Pour over the dressing and toss through gently.

6 Serve immediately on a bed of fresh rocket or lettuce leaves.

COOK'S TIP
Wheatberries take nearly twice as long to cook compared to the other grains so need to be prepared separately.

VARIATIONS
• Use other tangy fruits such as pomegranate seeds, grapefruit or little clementines in place of the orange.
• Serve this salad chilled if you prefer.

Nutritional Information:
Energy 520kcal/2177kJ; 16g; Carbohydrate 61g, of which sugars 4g; Fat 25g, of which saturates 3g; Cholesterol 7mg; Calcium 75mg; Fibre 5g; Sodium 361mg.

FISH AND MEAT DISHES

Adding quinoa to meat or fish helps to make it go further, both in terms of bulk and nutrition. The recipes in this chapter are packed with protein, essential amino acids, vitamins and minerals, and offer many ways to add this supergrain to your favourite type of meat or fish dish.

Of Venetian origin, carpaccio is the name given to a dish with raw meat or fish. Omega-3-rich tuna fish is perfect for this, here coated in seasoned quinoa and seared to retain its juices. Served on a bed of nutty Camargue rice, quinoa and curly kale, the dish is great for entertaining. The fish should marinate for at least 3 hours in advance if possible.

SEARED TUNA CARPACCIO

SERVES 4
4 fresh tuna steaks, about 500g/1¼lb total weight
50g/2oz/⅓ cup cooked red quinoa
a handful of chopped fresh oregano
15ml/1 tbsp vegetable oil
15ml/1 tbsp sesame oil
salt and ground black pepper

For the marinade
45ml/3 tbsp horseradish sauce
juice of 1 lime
5ml/1 tsp Dijon mustard
ground black pepper

For the Camargue rice
30ml/2 tbsp olive oil
2 shallots, peeled and finely diced
115g/4oz/generous ½ cup Camargue rice
750ml/1¼ pints/3 cups fish stock
175g/6oz/1 cup pearl quinoa
115g/4oz kale, washed and thinly sliced
salt and ground black pepper

To serve
60ml/4 tbsp mayonnaise mixed with
  5ml/1 tsp wholegrain mustard
lime wedges

1 Three hours before eating, if possible, make the marinade by mixing the ingredients together in a medium-sized deep bowl. Add the tuna steaks, toss well to coat, cover and refrigerate.

2 Half an hour before you want to eat, prepare the rice and quinoa mixture. In a medium pan heat 15ml/1 tbsp olive oil, add the shallots and rice and cook for 3–4 minutes, until the shallot is soft.

3 Add the fish stock to the pan, bring to the boil and simmer for 25 minutes, then add the rinsed pearl quinoa and simmer for a further 15 minutes until both grains are al dente. Add a little water if necessary during cooking. Drain when cooked and set aside.

4 While the rice and quinoa mixture is cooking, prepare the marinated tuna.

5 Place the cooked red quinoa in a medium bowl and mix in the fresh oregano, a little salt and plenty of black pepper. Dip in the moist tuna steaks and evenly coat on all sides.

6 Heat a griddle if you have one, or heat the vegetable oil in a frying pan, and sear the coated steaks on a medium high heat for 1 minute until the coating is crisp. Turn over and cook the other side for a further 1 minute, then remove from the griddle or pan.

7 Using a sharp knife, slice the steaks into 5mm/¼in slices. Drizzle with the sesame oil, cover and set aside.

8 Fry the sliced kale in 15ml/1 tbsp olive oil with a sprinkling of water on high heat, stirring, for 2–3 minutes until wilted. Add the rice and grain mixture to the pan and stir into the kale to warm through. Taste, and season if necessary.

9 To serve, divide the rice, quinoa and kale mix between four plates and cover with slices of tuna. Top with a spoonful of mustard mayonnaise and serve with lime wedges for squeezing over.

Nutritional Information: Gluten free
Energy 686kcal/2878kJ; Protein 39g; Carbohydrate 63g, of which sugars 7g; Fat 33g, of which saturates 5g; Cholesterol 45mg; Calcium 122mg; Fibre 5g; Sodium 617mg.

Sumac comes from the berries of a shrub that grows in Africa and North America. It has a rich red colour and adds a lovely tangy flavour to food. Here, it offsets the rich oiliness of trout, which is stuffed with quinoa, dried fruit and herbs. This dish looks impressive but is deceptively easy to make. Serve any leftover stuffing with the fish.

QUINOA-STUFFED TROUT

SERVES 4
30ml/2 tbsp olive oil
1 medium onion, finely diced
1 clove garlic, crushed
30ml/2 tbsp sumac
2.5ml/½ tsp ground cinnamon
550ml/18fl oz/2½ cups fish stock
juice and rind of 1 lemon
175g/6oz/1 cup pearl quinoa
50g/2oz/⅓ cup finely chopped dried
  apricots
50g/2oz/⅓ cup raisins
4 small whole trout (about 1kg/2¼lb
  total weight), cleaned and descaled
salt and ground black pepper
finely cut lemon rind shreds, to garnish
roasted potatoes and green salad,
  to serve

1 Heat the oven to 180°C/350°F/Gas 4. Heat 15ml/1 tbsp of the olive oil in a medium pan and add the onion, garlic, sumac and cinnamon.

2 Fry for a few minutes to soften the onion and release the spice flavours. Add the stock to the pan with the lemon juice and rind, and stir in the quinoa.

3 Bring to the boil and simmer for 8 minutes. Add the apricots and raisins, and simmer for a further few minutes until the quinoa is cooked and the fruit plump. Season to taste.

4 Pat the fish dry with kitchen paper. Brush the skin with the remaining oil and lay the whole fish on a board to enable stuffing. Fill each fish with the fruited quinoa mix. Place the fish in a serving dish and cover with foil.

5 Bake for 20–30 minutes, until the fish is light pink and flaky. Dry-fry leftover stuffing in a frying pan to reheat.

6 Garnish the fish with lemon rind shreds and serve with the reheated stuffing, roasted potatoes and salad.

VARIATION
Use other oily fish, such as mackerel and salmon, depending on availability.

Nutritional Information: Gluten free with GF fish stock
Energy 478kcal/2008kJ; Protein 37g; Carbohydrate 45g, of which sugars 18g; Fat 18g, of which saturates 3g; Cholesterol 98mg; Calcium 97mg; Fibre 7g; Sodium 494mg.

This luxurious pie became popular in Russia in the early part of the 20th century and could contain cod, sturgeon, cabbage, and rice. Here, the traditional rice layer has been replaced with protein-rich red quinoa, which beautifully complements the deep-pink salmon and makes an impressive centrepiece for a celebratory meal.

SALMON AND QUINOA COULIBIAC

SERVES 4
400g/14oz salmon fillet
15ml/1 tbsp olive oil
1 medium onion, finely chopped
75g/3oz/scant 1 cup mushrooms, finely chopped
1 clove garlic, crushed
115g/4oz/²/₃ cup red quinoa
350ml/12fl oz/1½ cups fish stock
2 eggs
120ml/4fl oz/½ cup white wine
a good handful of fresh parsley, chopped
juice and rind of 1 lemon
350g/12oz all-butter puff pastry
salt and ground black pepper
30ml/2 tbsp mix of milk and melted butter, to glaze

1 Place the salmon fillets on a baking tray and part-cook under a medium grill (broiler) for 5 minutes on each side. Remove the skin. Flake the flesh, removing any bones, and set aside.

2 Heat the olive oil in a pan, add the chopped onion, mushrooms, garlic and rinsed quinoa and cook for 2–3 minutes until the onions start to brown.

3 Add the fish stock, then the whole eggs in their shells. Cover and simmer for 8 minutes to hard-boil the eggs.

4 Remove the eggs with a slotted spoon and place in cold water. Add the wine to the quinoa broth and continue cooking until most of the liquid has been absorbed and the quinoa is tender.

5 Add the chopped parsley, grated lemon rind and juice to the quinoa mixture, season with plenty of salt and pepper and set aside to cool. Preheat the oven to 200°C/400°F/Gas 6. Peel and roughly chop the cooked eggs.

6 Roll out the pastry into a large rectangle, making sure that you have a baking tray long enough to fit its length. Cut off a small amount to make decorative leaves or shapes if you wish.

7 Cut the pastry lengthways into two halves, one slightly wider than the other. Use a rolling pin to carefully move the larger half on to a baking tray (there is no need to grease this).

8 Evenly spread the flaked salmon down the middle of the pastry, leaving a margin along all four sides. Pile the quinoa mix over the salmon, shaping it evenly to make a rounded shape. Top with the chopped eggs.

9 Moisten the edge of the pastry with some of the milk and butter mixture, then carefully lift the other piece of pastry over the top without disturbing the filling. Press the edges together to seal, then use your fingers and a sharp knife to crimp the edges.

10 Decorate with pastry shapes if you wish. Glaze the coulibiac with the milk and butter mixture using a brush. Finally, make a couple of clean slits (about 2cm/¾in long) on the top.

11 Bake the coulibiac in the oven for 25–30 minutes, until the pastry is golden and brown. Serve hot, in slices.

....
Nutritional Information:
Energy 797kcal/2994kJ; Protein 32g; Carbohydrate 57g, of which sugars 7g; Fat 39g, of which saturates 3g; Cholesterol 114mg; Calcium 134mg; Fibre 5g; Sodium 519mg.

This is a dish in which Asia meets South America with mouthwatering effect. The stir-fry is a tangy mix of hot, sweet and salty flavours that brings the mild-tasting quinoa, egg and prawns to life. Here, supergrain quinoa adds a nutritious punch to a protein-rich, one-pan meal that will make a quick, easy and memorable supper.

CHINESE PRAWNS WITH EGG-FRIED QUINOA

SERVES 4

450g/1lb cooked, peeled king prawns (jumbo shrimp)
30ml/2 tbsp sesame oil
60ml/4 tbsp vegetable oil
1 medium chilli, finely chopped
2 cloves garlic, crushed
6 spring onions (scallions), finely sliced
250g/9oz/2 cups mushrooms, finely sliced
125g/5oz/1¼ cups frozen peas
600g/1lb 6oz/4 cups cooked white quinoa
6 eggs, beaten
prawn (shrimp) crackers, to serve

For the marinade
120ml/4fl oz/½ cup soy sauce
30ml/2 tbsp sesame seed oil
60ml/4 tbsp sweet chilli oil

1 Make the marinade by mixing all of the ingredients in a medium pan, add the prawns, tossing to coat, then cover with clear film (plastic wrap) and set aside to marinate for at least 2 hours.

2 Prepare all the rest of the ingredients before you begin, then heat the sesame and vegetable oils on high heat in a large frying pan or wok. Add the chopped chilli and garlic and stir-fry for 3–4 seconds to release the aromas.

3 Add the spring onions, mushrooms and peas to the pan, and stir-fry for a few minutes until the mushrooms are golden. Add the cooked quinoa and toss to heat through.

4 Meanwhile, place the marinade pan on high heat and cook the prawns in the marinade for 5 minutes.

5 Make a well in the centre of the stir-fried mixture and pour in the beaten eggs, allowing the heat to start cooking them from underneath for a couple of minutes.

6 Lower the heat slightly and quickly mix the semi-cooked egg with the other ingredients to finish cooking for a few seconds. Do not overcook or the egg will become rubbery.

7 Quickly add the prawns and marinade to the mixture and remove the pan from the heat.

8 Serve the stir-fry immediately in large bowls, accompanied by prawn crackers, if you wish.

VARIATION

Use cooked chicken instead of prawns (shrimp). Make sure it is thoroughly reheated at stage 4.

Nutritional Information: Gluten free with GF soy sauce Energy 691kcal/2741kJ; Protein 39g; Carbohydrate 40g, of which sugars 8g; Fat 40g, of which saturates 7g; Cholesterol 192mg; Calcium 169mg; Fibre 8g; Sodium 2766mg.

The aromatic flavours of Thai spices and herbs give quinoa the lift and twist that it needs. Black quinoa has a firmer texture than white, and has a striking inky colour and an earthy flavour, which complements the pale, opaque scallops. This dish is ideal either as a simple supper or as part of a Thai meal for entertaining.

THAI SCALLOPS WITH BLACK CHILLI QUINOA

SERVES 4
275g/10oz fresh scallops
3 spring onions (scallions), finely sliced
1 red (bell) pepper, finely chopped
15ml/1 tbsp sesame oil

For the marinade
15ml/1 tbsp sesame oil
25g/1oz fresh root ginger, grated
1/2 banana shallot, peeled and
  finely diced
5ml/1 tsp finely chopped lemon grass
5ml/1 tsp tamarind paste
45ml/3 tbsp ketjap manis (sweet
  soy sauce)
2 garlic cloves, crushed

For the black chilli quinoa
275g/10oz/1²/₃ cups black quinoa
400ml/14fl oz/1²/₃ cups coconut milk
600ml/1 pint/2¹/₂ cups water
1/2 banana shallot, finely chopped
1/2 fresh red chilli, finely chopped
fresh coriander (cilantro), to garnish
prawn (shrimp) crackers, to serve

1 First make the marinade. Place all of the ingredients into a mini blender and process until they form a coarse paste. Alternatively, blend them together using a mortar and pestle.

2 Place the scallops, spring onions and red pepper in a large bowl and add the marinade. Cover and set aside to marinate for at least 1 hour.

3 Prepare the chilli quinoa. Rinse the quinoa in water, then transfer to a pan.

4 Add the coconut milk, water, shallot and chilli to the pan. Bring the quinoa to the boil, cover, reduce the heat and simmer for 12–14 minutes, until the quinoa is cooked but firm. Drain, reserving any excess liquid, and set aside.

5 When you are ready to serve, heat the sesame oil in a wok or large frying pan. Add the scallops, vegetables and marinade and stir-fry for 3–5 minutes on a high heat, until the scallops are cooked and fragrant, the vegetables softened and the liquid evaporated. Add the quinoa to the pan and toss around to warm through.

6 Divide the quinoa and scallop mixture between four bowls, then pour over the warmed reserved juices from cooking the quinoa. Garnish with fresh coriander and serve straight away.

VARIATION
Use fresh king prawns (jumbo shrimp) in place of the scallops.

COOK'S TIP
Be careful not to overcook the scallops or they will lose their characteristic tender texture and become rubbery.

Nutritional Information: Gluten free with GF soy sauce
Energy 422kcal/1742kJ; Protein 25g; Carbohydrate 55g, of which sugars 10g; Fat 12g, of which saturates 2g; Cholesterol 26mg; Calcium 138mg; Fibre 6g; Sodium 854mg.

Quinoa is an excellent gluten-free stuffing ingredient in place of breadcrumbs. If used in place of sausagemeat it also lowers the fat content. This recipe uses the traditional flavourings of lemon, sage and onion to bring out the delicious taste of roast chicken, while the quinoa-coated vegetables are the perfect accompaniment.

LEMON AND QUINOA-STUFFED ROAST CHICKEN

SERVES 4
1 x 1.3kg/3lb whole chicken
15ml/1 tbsp olive oil
4 rashers (strips) streaky (fatty) bacon
salt and ground black pepper

For the stuffing
15ml/1 tbsp vegetable oil
2 cloves garlic, crushed
1 medium onion, finely chopped
125g/4¼oz/¾ cup pearl quinoa
475ml/16fl oz/2 cups water
2 lemons, juice of both, grated rind of 1
25g/1oz/¼ cup quinoa flour
25g/1oz fresh sage, finely chopped
25g/1oz capers, roughly chopped
25g/1oz/⅙ cup butter
salt and ground black pepper

For the roast vegetables
600g/1lb 6oz mixed root vegetables
   (beetroot (beet), swede (rutabaga),
   sweet potato, parsnip, celeriac),
   peeled and cut into 4cm/1½in batons
25g/1oz/¼ cup quinoa flour
15ml/1 tbsp fresh parsley, chopped
30ml/2 tbsp olive oil
salt and ground black pepper

1 Heat the oven to 200°C/400°F/Gas 6. Prepare the stuffing. Heat the oil in a pan and add the garlic, onion, quinoa and water. Bring to the boil, and simmer for 12–14 minutes, until the quinoa is soft to bite. Drain off any excess water. Mix in the remaining stuffing ingredients and plenty of salt and pepper.

2 Loosely stuff the neck cavity of the chicken two-thirds full; heat must be able to circulate inside the bird. Weigh the stuffed chicken and calculate the cooking time based on 20 minutes per 450g/1lb plus 10–20 minutes, and then 30 minutes resting time.

3 Brush the outside of the chicken with olive oil, season with salt and pepper and cover with bacon rashers. Place in the hot oven for 20 minutes, then baste with the juices and reduce the temperature to 190°C/375°F/Gas 5.

4 Par-boil the root vegetables for about 3 minutes in a covered pan. Drain, add the quinoa flour, parsley and salt and pepper, toss to coat and set aside.

5 About 20 minutes before the end of the chicken's cooking time, place the olive oil for the roast vegetables in an ovenproof casserole and heat. Remove the bacon from the top of the chicken, set aside, and baste the chicken.

6 Add the quinoa-coated vegetables to the hot casserole, turning to coat in the oil, then place in the oven.

7 When the chicken is cooked, test by inserting a skewer into the thickest part of the thigh and checking that the juices run clear, remove from the oven and set aside, covered, to rest.

8 Increase the oven temperature to 200°C/400°F/Gas 6 and roast the vegetables for 15 minutes, until crispy.

9 Carve the chicken and serve with the crispy bacon, a spoonful of stuffing and the quinoa-coated roast vegetables.

Nutritional Information: Gluten free
Energy 778kcal/3257kJ; Protein 56g; Carbohydrate 50g, of which sugars 12g; Fat 41g, of which saturates 11g; Cholesterol 186mg; Calcium 161mg; Fibre 8g; Sodium 878mg.

This tagine-style casserole of spiced meat and vegetables is packed with North African flavours. It is marvellous as a delicious one-pot meal for many hungry mouths, and is nutritionally well balanced since it contains three protein sources (chicken, chickpeas and quinoa), as well as carbohydrate and a generous amount of vegetables.

MOROCCAN CHICKEN CASSEROLE

SERVES 4

30ml/2 tbsp vegetable oil
450g/1lb chicken thighs, skinned
6 shallots, peeled and cut in half
2 garlic cloves, crushed
2.5cm/1in piece of fresh root ginger, grated
5ml/1 tsp ground ginger
7.5ml/1½ tsp smoked paprika
7.5ml/1½ tsp ground cumin
225g/8oz butternut squash, peeled and cut into 2cm/¾in cubes
300g/12oz/2 cups pearl quinoa
115g/4oz/scant 1 cup cooked chickpeas
200g/7oz canned cherry tomatoes
50g/2oz/½ cup black olives, pitted
1 preserved lemon, finely chopped
25g/1oz/¼ cup raisins
30ml/2 tbsp tomato purée (paste)
1.2 litres/2 pints/5 cups chicken stock
salt and ground black pepper
a handful of roughly torn fresh coriander (cilantro), to garnish
chunks of fresh bread, to serve

1 Heat the oven to 180°C/350°F/Gas 4. Heat 15ml/1 tbsp of the vegetable oil in a large frying pan and add the chicken thighs, sealing them over a high heat for a few minutes until lightly browned all over. Transfer to a large lidded casserole.

2 Add a further 15ml/1 tbsp oil to the frying pan and add the shallots, garlic, fresh and ground ginger, paprika, cumin and butternut squash. Fry for around 5–6 minutes to release the flavours and soften the vegetables.

3 Add the quinoa, chickpeas, tomatoes, olives, lemon and raisins and stir to heat through and coat the quinoa. Transfer the mixture to the casserole, then place over medium heat.

4 Add the tomato purée, stock and seasoning to the casserole and bring to a simmer, then cover and cook in the oven for 50–60 minutes, until the squash is tender and most of the juices have been absorbed by the quinoa. Remove the casserole from the oven and stir in the fresh coriander.

5 Serve in warmed bowls with chunks of fresh bread. Don't leave this to stand for too long, as the quinoa will continue to absorb the cooking liquid.

VARIATION
Stir 15ml/1 tbsp clear honey into the mixture just before serving for a less spicy, sweeter dish.

COOK'S TIP
This dish can be made in advance, but it may need a little more stock stirring through before being served, as the quinoa will absorb any available liquid while it stands.

Nutritional Information:
Energy 678kcal/2846kJ; Protein 36g; Carbohydrate 72g, of which sugars 16g; Fat 30g, of which saturates 6g; Cholesterol 123mg; Calcium 162mg; Fibre 7g; Sodium 739mg.

These delicious little morsels contain Chinese five-spice powder, a warm, pungent mix that includes star anise and cinnamon. The key to speedy preparation is having some cooked quinoa handy. The patties are great for a quick supper dish or a sizzling summer barbecue, served with pak choi and cooked quinoa with shallots and garlic.

FIVE-SPICE PORK AND APPLE PATTIES

SERVES 4
vegetable oil, for frying
1 medium onion, finely chopped
2 cloves garlic, crushed
1 medium cooking apple, peeled, cored and grated
450g/1lb minced (ground) lean pork
10ml/2 tsp Chinese five-spice powder
5ml/1 tsp mustard
115g/4oz/²/₃ cup cooked red or black quinoa
1 egg, beaten
50g/2oz/¹/₂ cup quinoa flour
salt and ground black pepper
shallot and garlic quinoa (see Cook's Tip), steamed pak choi (bok choy) and soy sauce, to serve

1 Heat 15ml/1 tbsp oil in a medium frying pan. Add the onion, garlic and apple and fry for 3–4 minutes, until softened. Remove from the heat and transfer to a large bowl.

2 Add the minced pork, five-spice powder and mustard to the bowl, together with the cooked quinoa, beaten egg, flour and seasoning. Use your hands to mix the ingredients together until well combined.

3 With slightly dampened hands, to help prevent sticking, shape the mixture into eight burger-size 'patties' and set them aside on a floured board.

4 Wash and dry the frying pan, heat 30ml/2 tbsp oil in the pan and fry the patties on high heat for 3–4 minutes.

5 Flip the patties and fry on the other side for another 3 minutes, then reduce the heat and cook for a further 6–8 minutes, until cooked through and no longer pink in the middle. Keep warm in the oven.

6 Serve the patties on a pile of quinoa (see Cook's Tip), with steamed pak choi and a dash of soy sauce.

VARIATIONS
• To make beefburgers use minced (ground) beef instead of pork, and grated carrot instead of apple.
• You can omit the spices and flavour with mixed chopped herbs if you wish.
• Alternatively, brush the uncooked patties with a little oil and cook on a hot barbecue.

COOK'S TIP
To make the quinoa accompaniment, cook the required amount of quinoa and, while it is steaming, fry a finely chopped banana shallot on high heat until golden and crispy. Add a crushed garlic clove and stir for a few seconds to release the aroma, then stir the onion and garlic mixture into the cooked quinoa, adding salt and pepper to taste.

Nutritional information per patty: Gluten free
Energy 766kcal/3167kJ; Protein 16g; Carbohydrate 22g, of which sugars 6g; Fat 69g, of which saturates 24g; Cholesterol 113mg; Calcium 70mg; Fibre 3g; Sodium 105mg.

This is a Middle Eastern-inspired rice dish that is often made using lamb and flavoured with spices. Here, black quinoa replaces the rice, and is cooked in a rich, spicy tomato stock with colourful vegetables to make a striking dish. Black quinoa retains its bite more than pearl quinoa, so is perfect for this recipe, where texture definition is needed.

LAMB AND BLACK QUINOA PILAFF

SERVES 4

2.5ml/½ tsp coriander seeds
5ml/1 tsp cumin seeds
15ml/1 tbsp olive oil
1 medium onion, finely diced
300g/11oz minced (ground) lamb
1 clove garlic, peeled and crushed
1 small aubergine (eggplant), chopped
1 red (bell) pepper, chopped
25g/1oz/¼ cup pitted black olives
275g/10oz/1⅔ cups black quinoa
250ml/8fl oz/1 cup water
450g/1lb canned chopped tomatoes
30ml/2 tbsp tomato purée (paste)
1 lamb or chicken stock (bouillon) cube
3 cardamom pods, bruised
2 bay leaves
salt and ground black pepper
natural (plain) yogurt, Seeded
    Flatbread (see pages 90–1) and
    green salad with lemon juice,
    to serve

1 In a small pan, dry-fry the coriander and cumin seeds on high heat for 1–2 minutes to release their flavours. Grind using a mortar and pestle or whizz briefly in a coffee grinder.

2 Add the oil and onion to a large frying pan and fry for 3 minutes on medium heat to soften the onion.

3 Add the lamb to the pan and fry on high heat for 3–4 minutes before adding the ground seeds, garlic, aubergine, pepper and olives.

4 Stir-fry for another 3–4 minutes. The lamb juices released will be absorbed by the aubergine, but you could drain them off for a less fatty dish, if you wish.

5 Add the rinsed quinoa, water, tomatoes, tomato purée, stock cube, cardamom pods and bay leaves to the pan, season well with salt and pepper.

6 Bring to the boil, reduce the heat and simmer for 20 minutes until most of the liquid is absorbed and the quinoa is soft but still with some bite.

7 Leave the pilaff to stand for about 5–10 minutes before serving. Remove the bay leaves, and the cardamom pods if you can find them.

8 Serve the pilaff drizzled with natural yogurt to offset the naturally rich lamb, along with Seeded Flatbread and crisp salad leaves, dressed with lemon juice.

COOK'S TIP
You can use pearl quinoa in this recipe, but reduce the cooking time to 15 minutes and the standing time to no longer than 5 minutes to avoid the quinoa swelling too much.

VARIATION
Use lamb shoulder cut into 1cm/½in dice instead of minced (ground) meat.

Nutritional Information:
Energy 488kcal/2042kJ; Protein 28g; Carbohydrate 54g, of which sugars 12g; Fat 19g, of which saturates 6g; Cholesterol 57mg; Calcium 152mg; Fibre 8g; Sodium 560mg.

VEGETARIAN MAINS

Quinoa is perhaps one of the most perfect non-animal sources of protein, containing all nine essential amino acids, as well as vital nutrients, iron, calcium and B vitamins. As the recipes in this chapter show, quinoa really comes into its own as the main ingredient in vegetarian dishes.

Laksa is a Malay/Singaporean curry of which there are many variants. Most recipes use either prawns, tofu or chicken, as well as crisp vegetables, vermicelli noodles and fragrant spices, all served in a coconut milk base. Here the noodles are substituted with pearl quinoa to create a substantial and mouthwatering lunch or supper dish.

MALAYSIAN TOFU AND QUINOA LAKSA

SERVES 4

10ml/2 tbsp vegetable oil
10ml/2 tbsp red curry paste
150g/5oz sweet potato, peeled and cubed
125g/4¼oz/¾ cup pearl quinoa
300ml/½ pint/1¼ cups coconut milk
600ml/1 pint/ 2 cups water
15ml/1 tbsp tamarind paste
1 clove garlic, crushed
25g/1oz spring onions (scallions), sliced into 5mm/¼in slices
8 mangetouts (snow peas)
4 baby corn, cut in half
200g/7oz tofu, cut into 2cm/¾in square cubes
fresh coriander (cilantro), chopped, and a 6cm/2½in piece of cucumber cut into thin matchsticks, to garnish
green tea, to serve

1 Heat 15ml/1 tbsp oil in a large pan, then add the curry paste, sweet potato cubes and quinoa. Fry on medium heat for 3–4 minutes, until the spice fragrances and flavours are released.

2 Add the coconut milk to the pan and stir until smooth, then add the water and tamarind paste. Bring to the boil, then lower the heat and simmer for 12–14 minutes, stirring occasionally, until the quinoa is tender.

3 Drain the quinoa, cover to keep warm and set aside, reserving the curried coconut stock in a small pan. Do not leave the quinoa in the stock or it will continue to absorb the fluid and swell.

4 In a frying pan, heat the remaining oil and add the garlic, spring onions, mangetouts and baby corn. Stir-fry on high heat for 3–4 minutes, until softened but still crisp.

5 Add the tofu cubes to the frying pan and sear for a further 3 minutes, gently turning the cubes only once or twice to avoid breaking them. Reheat the coconut stock.

6 To serve, divide the tofu and vegetables and the quinoa mixture between four large warmed bowls, and pour over the hot stock. Garnish with fresh coriander leaves and cucumber matchsticks. Serve with green tea to cool your senses.

COOK'S TIPS
• Key to this recipe is keeping the vegetables crisp and the tofu intact to give a curry with well-defined shapes and texture.
• You can make the curry in advance so long as you separate the quinoa from the coconut stock, or it will absorb the liquid, leaving you with quinoa risotto.

Nutritional Information: Gluten free
Energy 266kcal/1121kJ; Protein 12g; Carbohydrate 38g, of which sugars 12g; Fat 8g, of which saturates 1g; Cholesterol 0mg; Calcium 264mg; Fibre 4g; Sodium 152mg.

This is an economical and complete one-pot meal, since it contains protein, carbohydrate and vegetables. It is also quick and easy to make, and even more sustaining when served with the flatbread. Rich in iron and calcium from lentils, spinach and quinoa you will receive a nutritional as well as a flavour boost.

QUINOA AND LIME CURRY WITH SEEDED FLATBREAD

SERVES 4
15ml/1 tbsp rapeseed (canola) oil
1 small onion, finely sliced
1 clove garlic, peeled and crushed
15ml/1 tbsp garam masala
115g/4oz cauliflower florets
1 medium carrot, peeled and diced
125g/4¼oz/¾ cup pearl quinoa
150g/5oz/generous ½ cup red lentils
750ml/1¼ pints/3 cups boiling water
400g/14oz canned chopped tomatoes
15ml/1 tbsp tomato purée (paste)
115g/4oz spinach, washed and
  shredded
15ml/1 tbsp fresh coriander (cilantro),
  chopped, plus extra for garnishing
30ml/2 tbsp lime pickle
salt and ground black pepper
lime wedges and lime pickle, to serve

For the seeded flatbreads
30ml/2 tbsp mixed seeds, such as
  pumpkin, sunflower and poppy
175g/6oz/1½ cups wholemeal
  (whole-wheat) flour
175g/6oz/1½ cups quinoa flour
7.5ml/1½ tsp baking powder
10ml/2 tsp ground cumin

2.5ml/½ tsp salt
30ml/2 tbsp olive oil
about 175ml/6fl oz/¾ cup cold water
vegetable oil, for frying

1 Make the flatbread dough. Toast the seeds for 4–5 minutes under a medium grill (broiler) or in a dry frying pan.

2 Combine the seeds with the flours, baking powder, cumin and salt in a large bowl. Add the oil and enough water to make a smooth, pliable dough; you may not need all the water. Knead lightly, cover with a dish towel and set aside.

3 Make the curry. Heat the oil in a large pan, add the onion, garlic and garam masala and fry on medium heat for a few minutes to release the spice flavours. Add the cauliflower and carrot and fry for 3–4 minutes to soften.

4 Add the quinoa, lentils, water, chopped tomatoes and tomato purée to the pan and bring to the boil. Reduce the heat and simmer for 15 minutes until the quinoa and lentils are cooked.

5 Stir in the spinach, coriander and lime pickle and cook for 2 minutes more.

6 Meanwhile, halve the flatbread dough and roll out very thinly (about 5mm/¼in in thickness). Heat a little oil in a frying pan, and fry one on medium heat for 3–4 minutes, until it blisters and starts to singe slightly. Flip over and cook on the other side. Remove from the heat, cut into wedges or strips, and fold in a clean dish towel to keep the bread warm and soft. Repeat with the remaining dough.

7 Check the curry for seasoning, then divide between four bowls, garnish with coriander and serve with lime wedges, flatbread and some lime pickle.

VARIATIONS
Replace the cauliflower and carrot with other vegetables, if you wish. Try green beans and potato, or mushroom and courgette (zucchini).

Nutritional Information:
Energy 755kcal/1385kJ; Protein 30g; Carbohydrate 115g, of which sugars 12g; Fat 26g, of which saturates 5g; Cholesterol 0mg; Calcium 308mg; Fibre 10g; Sodium 460mg.

The tangy sweet and sour flavours of a Chinese-style stir-fry bring quinoa to life. Mix and match the ingredients according to what is in season, but make sure everything you use is fresh, for the best taste and texture. The secret of a good stir-fry is to have all the ingredients ready, as once you begin to cook there's no time to prepare them.

CHINESE QUINOA AND VEGETABLE STIR-FRY

SERVES 4
175g/6oz/1 cup pearl quinoa
750ml/1¼ pints/3 cups water
10ml/2 tsp ground ginger
15ml/1 tbsp sugar
30ml/2 tbsp rice vinegar
60ml/4 tbsp vegetable stock
30ml/2 tbsp light soy sauce, plus extra
   for serving (optional)
2.5ml/½ tsp dried chilli flakes
15ml/1 tbsp vegetable oil
30ml/2 tbsp sesame oil
2 cloves garlic, peeled and crushed
2cm/1in piece of fresh root ginger,
   peeled and grated
1 carrot, peeled and cut into thin strips
1 orange or yellow (bell) pepper,
   deseeded and cut into thin strips
175g/6oz/generous 2 cups mushrooms,
   finely sliced
1 medium leek, washed and cut into
   5cm/2in long strips
2 sticks celery, cut into 5cm/2in
   long strips
150g/5oz beansprouts
150g/5oz broccoli, cut into small florets
75g/3oz cashew nuts, roughly chopped

1 Rinse the quinoa, then transfer to a pan, add the water and ground ginger and bring to the boil. Simmer for about 14–16 minutes, until tender to bite. Drain and set aside.

2 Meanwhile in a small bowl mix the sugar and vinegar, stirring until all of the sugar is dissolved. Add to this the stock, soy sauce and chilli flakes, then cover and set aside.

3 In a wok or large frying pan, heat the vegetable and sesame oils and add the garlic and grated fresh ginger, stirring briefly to release their aromas.

4 Add the carrot, pepper and mushrooms to the wok, fry for a few seconds and then add the leek, celery, beansprouts and broccoli. Fry again for a few seconds, tossing all the time.

5 Add the cashew nuts to the wok and again stir-fry, tossing regularly, for 5–7 minutes on high heat to lightly cook the raw vegetables without allowing them to get too soft.

6 Add the cooked quinoa to the wok and toss, still on a high heat, until heated through, then add the stock, soy sauce and vinegar mixture, stirring and tossing to combine as the liquid sizzles. Serve immediately, with extra soy sauce if you wish.

COOK'S TIP
The vegetables will look and cook best if they are cut into long thin strips (about 5mm x 5cm/¼ x 2in), and small broccoli florets.

VARIATIONS
Use other vegetables of your choice, such as fennel, pak choi (bok choy), asparagus and spring onions (scallions).

Nutritional Information: Gluten free with GF soy sauce Energy 500kcal/2091kJ; Protein17g; Carbohydrate 51g, of which sugars 16g; Fat 27g, of which saturates 4g; Cholesterol 0mg; Calcium 120mg; Fibre 6g; Sodium 686mg.

Quinoa makes a very pleasing change to traditional Italian arborio rice. Unlike risotto it doesn't need constant stirring between gradual additions of stock, so doesn't require undivided attention and instant serving. Topped with good-quality hard cheese, and served with a tomato and red onion salad, this is a winning winter comfort dish.

MUSHROOM QUINOA RISOTTO

SERVES 4
30ml/2 tbsp olive oil
300g/12oz/2 cups red quinoa
10 spring onions (scallions), finely sliced
3 cloves garlic, peeled and crushed
1 litre/1³/4 pints/4 cups vegetable stock
300g/11oz/4 cups chopped chestnut
   mushrooms
25g/1oz/2 tbsp butter
60ml/4 tbsp double (heavy) cream
115g/4oz Parmesan cheese shavings
salt and ground black pepper
fresh parsley, chopped, to garnish
red onion and tomato salad, to serve

1 Heat the oil in a heavy pan and add the quinoa, spring onions and garlic. Fry, stirring, for 3–4 minutes until softened.

2 Add half of the stock and bring to the boil. Lower the heat and simmer for about 5 minutes, stirring occasionally.

3 Add the chopped mushrooms to the pan with the remainder of the stock and cook for about 8–10 minutes, until the quinoa is soft but retains a little firmness for texture.

4 Add further boiling water if required to keep the risotto moist.

5 Stir in the butter, cream, salt if needed, and black pepper to taste. Serve on warmed plates, sprinkled with shaved Parmesan cheese and chopped parsley, and accompanied by a red onion and tomato salad.

Nutritional Information: Gluten free with GF stock
Energy 568kcal/2372kJ; Protein 22g; Carbohydrate 51g, of which sugars 6g; Fat 32g, of which saturates 14g; Cholesterol 57mg; Calcium 397mg; Fibre 7g; Sodium 535mg.

Jambalaya originated in the Caribbean and blends Spanish and local traditions. It usually contains meat and rice, but here quinoa and vegetables are cooked with stock and spices until tender. This medium-hot version uses chilli, paprika and cayenne pepper. Jambalaya is a meal in its own right, but could also be served a side dish with meat or fish.

BEAN CREOLE QUINOA JAMBALAYA

SERVES 4

30ml/2 tbsp vegetable oil
1 medium onion, roughly chopped
2 cloves garlic, crushed
1 medium fresh or dried chilli,
  finely chopped
5ml/1 tsp ground paprika
5ml/1 tsp ground cayenne pepper
1 red (bell) pepper, deseeded and cut
  into 1cm/½in wide strips
1 small aubergine (eggplant), washed,
  and cut into 1cm/½in wide slices
2 celery stick, chopped into
  1cm/½in pieces
2 medium tomatoes, washed and
  cut into wedges
115g/4oz/scant 1 cup drained canned
  butter (lima) beans
275g/10oz/1⅔ cups pearl quinoa
1 litre/1¾ pints/4 cups vegetable stock
15ml/1 tbsp tomato purée (paste)
2 bay leaves
salt and ground black pepper
60ml/4 tbsp sour cream and 30ml/2 tbsp
  grated cheese, to serve

1 Put the oil, onion, garlic, chilli and spices in a wide pan or casserole dish and fry for 4–5 minutes on medium heat to release the spicy flavours. Be careful not to over-brown the onion.

2 Add the pepper, aubergine and celery and heat with the spice mixture for a further 5 minutes, turning occasionally, until the vegetables start to soften. Add the tomatoes, butter beans, quinoa, stock, tomato purée, seasoning and bay leaves and bring to the boil.

3 Lower the heat and simmer for around 14–16 minutes, until the quinoa is tender to bite but there is still a little stock remaining.

4 To serve, remove the bay leaves and ladle the jambalaya into deep bowls. Drizzle each with a spoonful of sour cream and a sprinkling of grated cheese.

COOK'S TIP
Traditional jambalaya may be baked in the oven after it has been cooked on the stove. This is ideal if you want to make the dish in advance; simply add a further 120ml/4fl oz/½ cup stock, place in an ovenproof dish and bake for about 30 minutes in a medium oven at 180°C/350°F/Gas 4, covering if necessary to avoid dryness.

VARIATION
Other types of beans can be used – try canned black kidney beans for a striking colour contrast.

Nutritional Information:
Energy 464kcal/1939kJ; Protein 16g; Carbohydrate 62g, of which sugars 12g; Fat 18g, of which saturates 5g; Cholesterol 16mg; Calcium 167mg; Fibre 7g; Sodium 434mg.

This dish uses carbohydrate-rich root vegetables bathed in cream and Parmesan cheese, and contains a mouthwatering range of soft and crunchy textures and sweet and savoury flavours. Inspired by French dauphinois potatoes, it makes a great one-dish vegetarian main meal, and is also a pleasant change to potatoes for accompanying meat or fish.

VEGETABLES WITH A QUINOA AND CHEESE CRUST

SERVES 4

1 small onion, finely diced
1 clove garlic, crushed
15ml/1 tbsp vegetable oil
225g/8oz celeriac, peeled and diced into 1cm/½in cubes
225g/8oz sweet potato, peeled and diced into 1cm/½in cubes
225g/8oz parsnip, peeled and diced into 1cm/½in cubes
225g/8oz fresh beetroot (beet), peeled and very thinly sliced
175ml/6fl oz/¾ cup milk
5ml/1 tsp ground nutmeg
175ml/6fl oz/¾ cup double (heavy) cream
salt and ground black pepper
rocket (arugula) salad with a mustard dressing, to serve

For the quinoa and cheese crust
175g/6oz/1 cup cooked quinoa
75ml/5 tbsp grated Parmesan cheese
5ml/1 tsp mixed dried herbs
ground black pepper

1 Heat the oven to 190°C/375°F/Gas 5. In a large pan, soften the onion and garlic in the vegetable oil over medium heat for 3–4 minutes. Add the celeriac, sweet potato and parsnip and fry on medium heat for a further 3–4 minutes.

2 Add the milk to the pan, together with the nutmeg and seasoning, stir and then bring the milk to the boil. Cover, lower the heat and simmer for 7–8 minutes, until the vegetables are beginning to soften.

3 Stir the cream into the vegetables, then transfer to a shallow ovenproof dish and spread out evenly. Arrange the beetroot slices in a layer on top.

4 Make the quinoa and cheese crust by mixing together the ingredients in a bowl, with a good grinding of black pepper. Spread this evenly over the top of the beetroot layer.

5 Cover the dish with foil and bake in the oven for 20–25 minutes, until the vegetables are soft. Remove the foil and bake for a further 15 minutes to allow the crust to become crisp and golden.

6 Serve with a peppery rocket salad with a mustard dressing to contrast with the rich, creamy bake.

COOK'S TIP
Keeping the beetroot (beet) slices in a separate layer helps to retain the creamy colour of the sauce. Make sure that the slices are as thin as possible so that they cook completely in the oven.

VARIATION
Use grated blue cheese such as Stilton for the crust instead of Parmesan.

Nutritional Information: Gluten free
Energy 550kcal/2289kJ; Protein 16g; Carbohydrate 40g, of which sugars 17g; Fat 38g, of which saturates 21g; Cholesterol 85mg; Calcium 408mg; Fibre 9g; Sodium 352mg.

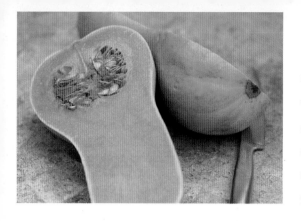

Quinoa lends itself perfectly as a stuffing for vegetables, with its excellent nutrient profile and ability to absorb exciting, vibrant flavours. Spanish smoked paprika dominates this spicy dish with its opulent taste and deep colour, and the finished dish is beautifully tempered by a sour cream drizzle and melted cheese.

STUFFED BUTTERNUT SQUASH

SERVES 4

1 large or 2 small butternut squash
  (about 800g/1¾lb total weight)
olive oil
30ml/2 tbsp pine nuts
30ml/2 tbsp roughly chopped hazelnuts
1 small onion, diced
1 clove garlic, crushed
5ml/1 tsp smoked paprika
200g/7oz chopped canned tomatoes
250ml/8fl oz/1 cup water
120ml/4fl oz/½ cup red wine
115g/4oz/⅔ cup black quinoa
75g/3oz/1 cup grated Parmesan cheese
salt and ground black pepper
90ml/6 tbsp sour cream and a pinch of
  smoked paprika, to garnish
mixed leaf salad, to serve

1 Preheat the oven to 190°C/375°F/Gas 5. Cut the butternut squash in half. Scrape away and discard the seeds and fibre.

2 Score two lines 4cm/1½in apart lengthways along the inside of the butternut squash, then slice under to remove this core section. Dice the extracted flesh into small cubes.

3 Place the squash halves in a roasting pan in the oven, inside facing up, season with salt and pepper and drizzle with olive oil. Bake for 15–20 minutes.

4 In the same oven, roast the butternut squash cubes in a separate roasting pan for 10 minutes until just tender, then add the pine nuts and hazelnuts and roast for a further 5 minutes until the pine nuts are golden. Set aside.

5 Meanwhile, heat 15ml/1 tbsp oil in a medium pan, add the onion, garlic and paprika and lightly fry for 5–8 minutes, until the onion is softened.

6 Add the tomatoes and their juice, the water, wine and quinoa to the onions and simmer for 13–15 minutes, until the quinoa is tender. Stir in the toasted nuts and season to taste with salt and plenty of ground black pepper.

7 Remove the pan from the heat. Stuff the cored cavity of the butternut squash halves, piling the excess on the top. Sprinkle with grated Parmesan cheese.

8 Cover with foil, transfer to the oven and bake for 10 minutes until the squash is cooked through. Remove the foil and bake for a further 5 minutes until the cheese is bubbling and golden.

9 Top the squash with a spoonful of sour cream and a pinch of sprinkled smoked paprika, and serve with a mixed leaf salad.

VARIATIONS
• Use this filling to stuff other vegetables of your choice, such as field (portobello) mushrooms, beefsteak tomatoes or courgettes (zucchini).
• You could also serve the stuffed squash with wilted greens, topped with hot fennel pangrattato (see page 104).

Nutritional Information: Gluten free
Energy 441kcal/1844kJ; Protein17g; Carbohydrate 40g, of which sugars 14g; Fat 22g, of which saturates 8g; Cholesterol 32mg; Calcium 400mg; Fibre 5g; Sodium 249mg.

A perennial classic, cheese soufflé is a light lunch or supper dish that is packed with protein from both the eggs and the cheese. This recipe includes useful carbohydrate and extra protein from quinoa as well as superfood broccoli, ensuring it provides a complete meal. Soufflés need to be taken from the oven straight to the table before they sink.

BROCCOLI AND STILTON QUINOA SOUFFLE

SERVES 4
200g/7oz broccoli, cut into small florets
50g/2oz/4 tbsp butter, plus extra
    for greasing
50g/2oz/½ cup quinoa flour
360ml/12fl oz/1½ cups milk
10ml/2 tsp wholegrain mustard
150g/5oz Stilton cheese, crumbled
75g/3oz/1 cup finely grated
    Parmesan cheese
125g/4¼oz/¾ cup pearl quinoa,
    cooked
8 eggs, separated
salt and ground black pepper
crisp green salad, to serve

1 Steam the broccoli florets in a small amount of water in a covered pan for about 2 minutes, until just tender but still retaining some bite. Drain well and set aside.

2 Butter a large, deep ovenproof dish (about 20cm/8in in diameter). Preheat the oven to 200°C/400°F/Gas 6.

3 Make a cheese sauce. Melt the butter in a heavy pan over low heat, stir in the quinoa flour to make a paste and cook for about 1 minute. Slowly add the milk, stirring continuously after each addition, to make a thick white sauce.

4 Remove the pan from the heat and add the mustard, crumbled Stilton and grated Parmesan and stir until melted. Season with a little salt and plenty of ground black pepper and set aside to cool slightly.

5 Beat the egg whites in a large bowl until stiff and foamy. Beat the egg yolks into the cheese sauce, making it smooth and glossy, then add the cooked quinoa.

6 Using a large metal spoon, fold the stiff egg whites into the cheesy sauce, keeping the movements quick and clean to try to avoid knocking out too much air, then stir in the broccoli florets.

7 Pour the soufflé into the greased dish and bake for about 20–25 minutes until golden and puffy. Take straight to the table, and serve with a crisp green salad.

COOK'S TIP
If you want to get ahead, you can prepare the broccoli and cheese sauce in advance. Gently heat the cheese sauce until it is just warm before adding the beaten egg whites and carrying on from step 5.

VARIATIONS
Try using mature (sharp) Cheddar cheese instead of Stilton and Parmesan, with cauliflower florets instead of the broccoli, or Manchego cheese with sun-dried tomatoes.

....
Nutritional Information: Gluten free.
Energy 537kcal/2229kJ; Protein 29g; Carbohydrate 17g, of which sugars 2g; Fat 39g, of which saturates 22g; Cholesterol 331mg; Calcium 446mg; Fibre 2g; Sodium 767mg.

This dish has a double quinoa hit with the pangrattato topping, replacing more traditional breadcrumbs, and also in the quinoa pasta. Pangrattato are flavoured, crisp breadcrumbs, used in Italian food to add texture and taste to pasta dishes. You can make a larger batch of this fiery quinoa version for adding a kick to salads or pasta dishes.

ROCKET QUINOA PASTA WITH PANGRATTATO

SERVES 4
400g/14oz quinoa pasta
15ml/1 tbsp olive oil
2 cloves garlic, crushed
75g/3oz rocket (arugula), roughly
  chopped
300ml/½ pint/1¼ cups crème fraîche
125g/4¼oz mozzarella balls
salt and ground black pepper

For the hot fennel pangrattato
30ml/2 tbsp chilli oil
5ml/1 tsp fennel seeds
2 cloves garlic, crushed
½ small dried chilli, crumbled
30ml/2 tbsp pine nuts
150g/5oz/scant 1 cup cooked
  white quinoa
salt and ground black pepper

1 First prepare the pangrattato. Heat the chilli oil in a small pan and add the spices, pine nuts and quinoa. Cook, stirring constantly, for 5–8 minutes until crisp and brown. Add salt and pepper to taste, then set aside.

2 Cook the pasta for about 15 minutes, or following the instructions on the packet, in a large pan of boiling water, stirring occasionally to prevent sticking.

3 Meanwhile make the pasta sauce. Heat the olive oil in a medium pan and add the garlic and rocket, cooking for 1–2 minutes until the rocket has wilted. Add the crème fraîche and heat until warmed through. Season with plenty of salt and pepper.

4 Lightly drain the cooked pasta and return to the pan, add the mozzarella balls and then stir in the hot sauce; the mozzarella should melt slightly but stay intact. Divide the pasta between four warmed bowls.

5 Sprinkle each serving with a teaspoon of pangrattato, serving the remainder in a small bowl at the table for people to help themselves.

COOK'S TIP
You can buy quinoa pasta, which both tastes like and is prepared in a similar way to regular pasta, in health food store or online.

VARIATIONS
• Tone down the pangrattato by adding less chilli, and using vegetable oil rather than chilli oil.
• You can toast the fennel seeds first, then crush them with a mortar and pestle for a stronger flavour if you wish.

Nutritional Information: Gluten free
Energy 931kcal/3893kJ; Protein 22g; Carbohydrate 94g, of which sugars 3g; Fat 55g, of which saturates 27g; Cholesterol 102mg; Calcium 244mg; Fibre 3g; Sodium 141mg.

These burgers use low-fat and fibre-rich canned black beans, which are a handy kitchen standby all year round. Combined with hot jalapeño peppers, chilli, lime and fresh coriander leaves, quinoa adds useful carbohydrate and contributes to a wholesome, rustic texture. Serve in burger buns, or with potato wedges and coleslaw.

SPICY BLACK BEAN BURGERS

SERVES 6
115g/4oz/²/₃ cup pearl quinoa
350ml/12fl oz/1½ cups water
30ml/2 tbsp vegetable oil
1 medium onion, finely chopped
1 stick celery, finely chopped
2 cloves garlic, crushed
6 jalapeño peppers, finely chopped
1 red or green chilli, finely chopped
2 medium carrots, peeled and grated
75g/3oz/½ cup roasted peanuts
1 lime, rind and juice
15ml/1 tbsp fresh coriander (cilantro), roughly chopped
400g/14oz can black beans, drained and rinsed
15ml/1 tbsp quinoa flour, for shaping
salt and ground black pepper
burger buns, shredded lettuce, sliced tomato and crème fraîche, to serve

1 Place the quinoa and water in a medium pan, bring to the boil and simmer for 15–17 minutes until soft.

2 In another pan heat 15ml/1 tbsp of the oil and add the onion, celery, garlic, jalapeños, chilli and salt and pepper.

3 Cook for 2–3 minutes on medium heat, then add the grated carrot and cook for 3 minutes. Leave to cool.

4 Blitz the cooked quinoa, peanuts, lime juice and rind, and coriander in a food processor. Add the beans to the and pulse a couple of times to incorporate.

5 Add the vegetable mixture to the processor and pulse briefly to combine. Test for seasoning. Shape into six burgers, handling lightly, and using quinoa flour as required to stop the mixture from sticking.

6 Fry the burgers in the remaining 15ml/1 tbsp oil, adding a little more if needed, and turning them halfway through cooking. Alternatively, spritz with oil and cook on a hot barbecue.

7 Serve in halved rolls with shredded lettuce, sliced tomato and crème fraîche.

....
Nutritional Information: Gluten free
Energy 296kcal/1243kJ; Protein 13g; Carbohydrate 33g, of which sugars 5g; Fat 14g, of which saturates 2g; Cholesterol 0mg; Calcium 55mg; Fibre 8g; Sodium 68mg.

These gently spiced fritters are easy to make and full of good things. Served with potato wedges, iron-rich watercress and a yogurt dressing, they make a great weekday supper. They are also very tasty served as a burger alternative in a bun, or as bitesize fritters rolled in a soft tortilla with salad and sliced peppers as a packed lunch.

QUINOA FRITTERS WITH SWEET POTATO WEDGES

SERVES 4
vegetable oil, for frying
1 medium onion, finely chopped
1 clove garlic, crushed
30ml/2 tbsp poppy seeds
10ml/2 tsp ground cumin
2.5ml/½ tsp ground turmeric
200g/7oz/generous 1 cup cooked pearl quinoa
1 medium courgette (zucchini), grated
1 medium carrot, peeled and grated
50g/2oz/²⁄₃ cup grated Parmesan cheese
75ml/5 tbsp crème fraîche or natural (plain) yogurt
30ml/2 tbsp quinoa flour, for coating
salt and ground black pepper
watercress, roughly torn, to serve

For the spicy sweet potato wedges
3 medium sweet potatoes, peeled and cut into thick wedges
30ml/2 tbsp olive oil
2.5ml/½ tsp paprika
2.5ml/½ tsp smoked paprika
a little cayenne pepper, optional
30ml/2 tbsp quinoa flour
salt and ground black pepper

For the yogurt dressing
30ml/2 tbsp olive oil
15ml/1 tbsp cider vinegar
60ml/4 tbsp natural (plain) yogurt
5ml/1 tsp Dijon mustard

1 Boil the sweet potato wedges in a pan of salted water for 5 minutes, then drain and transfer to a bowl. Preheat the oven to 200°C/400°F/Gas 6.

2 Add the oil, spices, quinoa flour and seasoning to the bowl and toss the potato wedges in the mixture. Spread in a roasting pan and cook in the oven for 20–25 minutes until golden and crispy, turning once halfway through cooking.

3 For the fritters, add 15ml/1 tbsp of the oil, the onion, garlic, poppy seeds and spices to a large frying pan and fry for 3–4 minutes, until the onion is soft.

4 Add the quinoa and grated vegetables to the onion mixture, and fry for a further 5–7 minutes until the vegetables are softened but the carrot still has a little bite.

5 Season with plenty of salt and black pepper and stir in the Parmesan cheese with the crème fraîche or yogurt to make a mouldable mixture. Transfer to a bowl and set aside until it is cool enough to handle.

6 Place the quinoa flour on a large plate and use your hands to make eight fritters, coating each one in quinoa flour once formed.

7 Whisk all the dressing ingredients together in a small bowl.

8 When the potatoes are nearly ready, heat enough oil in a frying pan to coat the bottom, and shallow-fry the fritters for 3–4 minutes on each side until lightly browned and crispy.

9 Serve the fritters hot, with the potato wedges, on a bed of watercress drizzled with the dressing.

....
Nutritional Information: Gluten free
Energy 577kcal/2398kJ; Protein 14g; Carbohydrate 41g, of which sugars 10g; Fat 45g, of which saturates 9g; Cholesterol 13mg; Calcium 394mg; Fibre 3g; Sodium 193mg.

DESSERTS
AND BAKES

Mainly seen as an ingredient for savoury dishes, quinoa is also ideal for baking, especially now that it comes in several different forms. Quinoa flour is, of course, gluten-free, and so desserts become more available for those with coeliac disease. In this chapter you will also find recipes made with pearl quinoa and quinoa flakes, for healthier and more sustaining puddings, desserts and tea-time treats.

Quinoa again shows true versatility here in a lovely, creamy milk-based dish. Rice desserts have been popular for centuries in the Middle East, Europe and Asia, where they have provided essential sustenance. In this version, pearl quinoa proves an effective substitute for pudding rice, sweetened and spiced with aromatic cardamom.

QUINOA PUDDING WITH CHERRY COMPOTE

SERVES 4

butter, for greasing
6 green cardamom pods
750ml/1¼ pint/3 cups milk
2.5ml/½ tsp ground cinnamon
115g/4oz/⅔ cup pearl quinoa
5ml/1 tsp vanilla extract
50g/2oz/¼ cup demerara (raw) sugar
60ml/4 tbsp double (heavy) cream

For the cherry compote

350g/12oz/1½ cups pitted fresh or
  frozen cherries
1 orange, strip of rind removed and
  then squeezed to provide about
  150ml/¼ pint/⅔ cup orange juice
50g/2oz/¼ cup caster (superfine) sugar
double (heavy) cream, to serve

1 Heat the oven to 190°C/375°F/Gas 5. Butter a medium ovenproof dish.

2 With the bottom of a rolling pin, crush the cardamom pods and extract the seeds with the tip of a sharp knife. Discard the husks, then grind the seeds in a mortar and pestle, or in a sturdy bowl with the bottom of the rolling pin.

3 Pour the milk into a large pan and add the ground cardamom seeds, cinnamon and quinoa. Bring to the boil, then reduce the heat to very low and gently simmer for 10 minutes to infuse the flavours and soften the quinoa.

4 Remove the pan from the heat and stir in the vanilla extract, sugar and cream, then pour into the prepared dish.

5 Add a little more milk to the mixture if necessary; it should still be loose before it is baked or it will become too dry and solid in the oven.

6 Bake in the oven for 15–20 minutes, until the top is golden brown and slightly crisp, but the inside is still soft and slightly wobbly.

7 Meanwhile, prepare the cherry compote. Place the cherries in a pan with the orange rind and juice, and the sugar. Bring to the boil and simmer for 15–20 minutes, until the mixture has a thick syrupy consistency.

8 To serve, divide the pudding between four dishes. Top with a spoonful of warm cherry compote and a drizzle of cream.

COOK'S TIP

You could also serve this pudding chilled, layering the milk pudding and the compote in tall dessert glasses, compote last, and topped with cream.

VARIATIONS

• Add a dash of Kirsch to the compote for a little added decadence.
• Substitute plums for the cherries.

Nutritional Information: Gluten free
Energy 460kcal/1933kJ; Protein 11g; Carbohydrate 69g, of which sugars 51g; Fat 17g, of which saturates 10g; Cholesterol 46mg; Calcium 279mg; Fibre 4g; Sodium 95mg.

A classic fruit crumble is a simple, satisfying and easy dessert to make, and this quinoa version makes a lovely, warming winter pudding. Star anise is often used in Chinese cuisine for savoury dishes, but here, combined with other spices, it adds a lovely warm note to the apple filling. Serve hot or cold, with whipped cream, for an indulgent dessert.

PEAR AND HAZELNUT CRUMBLE

SERVES 4
450g/1lb pears
75ml/5 tbsp apple juice
2 star anise
10ml/2 tsp mixed (apple pie) spice
15ml/1 tbsp caster (superfine) sugar
whipped cream or ice cream, to serve

For the crumble topping
75g/3oz/²/₃ cup quinoa flour
75g/3oz/³/₄ cup quinoa flakes
75g/3oz/6 tbsp soft butter, diced
75g/3oz/6 tbsp soft light brown
  sugar
50g/2oz hazelnuts, roughly chopped

1 Preheat the oven to 190°C/375°F/ Gas 5. Peel and core the pears, and cut into 2cm/³/₄in slices.

2 Place the pears in an ovenproof dish and add the apple juice, star anise, mixed spice and sugar, stirring to evenly coat the pears.

3 To make the crumble topping, place the quinoa flour and flakes into a large bowl and, using the tips of your fingers, rub in the soft butter until the mixture resembles coarse breadcrumbs. Use a fork to stir in the sugar and then the chopped hazelnuts.

4 Sprinkle the crumble mixture evenly over the spiced pears and bake for 25–30 minutes, until the crumble is browned and the pears feel soft when pierced with a sharp knife.

5 Serve the crumble hot with freshly whipped cream, custard, or ice cream.

VARIATIONS
• Use apples with the same spice mixture if you wish.
• Replace the star anise with 2–3 cloves if you prefer.
• You can also use rhubarb, but replace the star anise and mixed (apple pie) spice with 10ml/2 tsp ground ginger.

Nutritional Information: Gluten free
Energy 486kcal/2034kJ; Protein 7g; Carbohydrate 61g, of which sugars 37g; Fat 25g, of which saturates 11g; Cholesterol 9mg; Calcium 92mg; Fibre 3g; Sodium 123mg.

The original Brown Betty recipe, using breadcrumbs, originated in late 19th-century America, and was probably a frugal way of using up stale bread and windfall apples. The winning combination of apples, sugar and spices rarely fails, and this quinoa-rich recipe is no exception. Here quinoa flakes replace the breadcrumbs.

CRISP APPLE BROWN BETTY

SERVES 4
75g/3oz/6 tbsp butter, softened, plus extra for greasing
115g/4oz/1 cup quinoa flakes
50g/2oz/½ cup quinoa flour
75g/3oz/6 tbsp soft light brown sugar
5ml/1 tsp each of ground cinnamon, ground ginger and ground nutmeg
2.5ml/½ tsp ground cloves
4 medium cooking apples, cored, peeled and thinly sliced
crème fraîche or vanilla ice cream, to serve

1 Preheat the oven to 180°C/350°F/ Gas 4. Butter a deep, heatproof dish, approximately 18cm/7in in diameter.

2 In a large bowl rub the softened butter into a mixture of quinoa flakes and flour until the mixture resembles fine breadcrumbs. Stir in the sugar, cinnamon, nutmeg and ground cloves with a fork.

3 Place one third of the prepared apples in an even layer in the base of the prepared dish.

4 Sprinkle over a third of dry mixture and repeat the layers twice more, finishing with a layer of the dry mixture.

5 Cook in the oven for 20–30 minutes, until the apple is soft and the flake mixture is golden, reducing the temperature slightly if necessary to prevent it becoming too brown. Serve warm, with crème fraîche or ice cream.

VARIATION
Replace the apples with seasonal pears and dark (bittersweet) chocolate chips, if you prefer, layered with the spiced quinoa mixture.

Nutritional Information: Gluten free
Energy 470kcal/1969kJ; Protein 6g; Carbohydrate 60g, of which sugars 33g; Fat 24g, of which saturates 13g; Cholesterol 26mg; Calcium 78mg; Fibre 6g; Sodium 87mg.

The flavour and nuttiness of this dessert is transformed by simply toasting the quinoa, which adds to the delicious coffee taste. Although the result looks very impressive, a roulade isn't too difficult to make and can be done in advance, so delight your guests with this unusual gluten-free version of a classic cream roulade.

COFFEE AND ALMOND QUINOA ROULADE

SERVES 6

75g/3oz/½ cup quinoa
500ml/17fl oz/generous 2 cups water
4 eggs
150g/5oz/1¼ cup caster (superfine)
　sugar
75g/3oz/¾ cup ground almonds
25g/1oz/¼ cup cornflour (cornstarch)
5ml/1 tsp baking powder
caster (superfine) sugar, for rolling
30ml/2 tbsp flaked (sliced) almonds
fresh berries and coffee, to serve

For the coffee cream

300ml/½ pint/1¼ cups whipping cream
15ml/1 tbsp instant coffee dissolved in
　30ml/2 tbsp boiling water

1 Heat the oven to 180°C/350°F/Gas 4. Grease a 30 x 22cm/12 x 9in Swiss roll tin (jelly roll pan) and line the base and sides with baking parchment.

2 Spread the quinoa on a baking sheet and toast for 6–8 minutes under a medium grill (broiler) until golden. Place in a pan, add the water, bring to the boil and cook for 12–14 minutes, until soft.

3 Drain the quinoa if necessary and set aside to cool completely.

4 Whisk together the eggs and sugar, with an electric whisk, until light and frothy. Fold in the ground almonds, cornflour, cooled quinoa and baking powder using a large metal spoon.

5 Spread the mixture evenly over the base of the prepared tin and bake in the oven for 12–15 minutes, until golden brown, and springy when touched. Cover with a clean dish towel and allow to cool for 5–10 minutes.

6 Meanwhile, prepare the coffee cream. Whip the cream until firm but soft. Blend with the cooled, dissolved coffee and set aside in the refrigerator.

7 Dry-roast the almonds in a frying pan until lightly browned.

8 While the roulade is still slightly warm, cut a piece of baking parchment slightly larger than the sponge. Sprinkle with the almonds and 15ml/1 tbsp caster sugar.

9 Turn the roulade on to the sugary paper, and peel off the lining paper from the back. Make a shallow slit, without cutting all the way through the sponge, about 2cm/¾in in from one of the long edges. This makes rolling easier.

10 Carefully start to roll the roulade from the same side as the slit, making it as tight and straight as you can. The sugared paper should still be on the roll. Leave to cool completely.

11 When the sponge is completely cool unroll it, remove the sugared paper and spread the middle with coffee cream. Re-roll, arranging any dislodged flaked almonds on the top, and sprinkle with a little more caster sugar. Serve with fresh berries and coffee.

COOK'S TIP

Oiling the tin and baking parchment well is essential.

Nutritional Information: Gluten free
Energy 470kcal/1963kJ; Protein 7g; Carbohydrate 46g, of which sugars 34g; Fat 30g, of which saturates 13g; Cholesterol 51mg; Calcium 86mg; Fibre 1g; Sodium 23mg.

Everyone will eat these seemingly indulgent brownies with gusto, oblivious to the secret ingredient. Quinoa flour is particularly good in rich baked recipes as it is higher in fat than regular wheat flour. There are many ways to make brownies, most of which work well, but the key is always not to over-bake them or they lose their soft, moist insides.

MOCHA QUINOA BROWNIES

MAKES 10

225g/8oz plain (semisweet) chocolate
225g/8oz/1 cup butter
15ml/1 tbsp instant coffee granules
4 eggs
150g/5oz/1¼ cups quinoa flour
150g/5oz/1¼ cup muscovado (molasses) sugar
icing (confectioner's) sugar or unsweetened cocoa powder, for dusting
coffee, or ice cream and fresh berries, to serve

1 Heat the oven to 190°C/375°F/Gas 5 and line a 18 x 18cm/7 x 7in tin (pan) with oiled baking parchment.

2 Break the chocolate into squares and place in a heatproof bowl set over a pan of simmering water. Add the butter and instant coffee granules.

3 Heat the contents of the bowl until the chocolate melts, then stir until you have a velvety smooth chocolate mixture. Remove the bowl from the pan and set aside to cool slightly.

4 Beat the eggs, one at a time, into the cooled chocolate mixture, with a wooden spoon or balloon whisk, then use a metal spoon to fold in the flour and the sugar.

5 Pour the mixture into the prepared tin, smooth so it is evenly spread, then bang the tin gently on a work surface to get rid of any air pockets or gaps.

6 Bake in the oven for 15–20 minutes, until the brownies are firm at the edges but still soft in the middle.

7 Allow to cool in the tin for 10 minutes to make sure the middle sets, then cut into squares with a sharp knife. Leave to cool completely in the tin.

8 Dust the top liberally with either icing sugar or unsweetened cocoa powder and remove the brownies from the tin a square at a time.

9 Enjoy with a cup of coffee, or warm slightly and serve as a dessert with ice cream and fresh berries.

Nutritional Information: Gluten free with GF chocolate
Energy 413kcal/1725kJ; Protein 5g; Carbohydrate 41g, of which sugars 30g; Fat 27g, of which saturates 17g; Cholesterol 100mg; Calcium 37mg; Fibre 1g; Sodium 158mg.

Classic carrot cake should be moist and decadent and this recipe won't disappoint, helped by the addition of olive oil and a good proportion of grated carrot. This cake is gluten free so makes an eye-catching cake when alternative dietary requirements are being catered for. Serve with coffee, or with whipped cream for a decadent dessert.

FROSTED CARROT CAKE

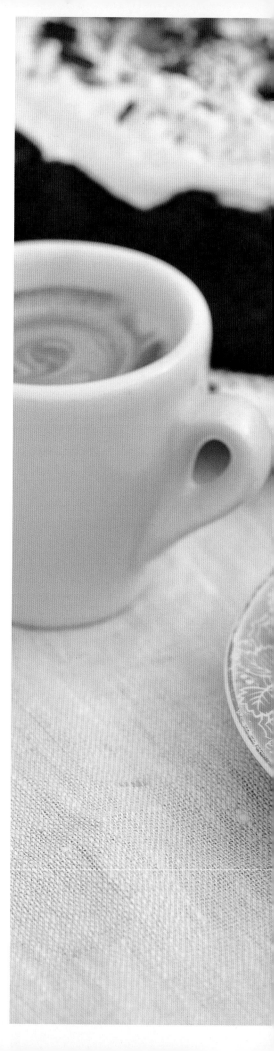

SERVES 10

175g/6oz/1¾ cup soft light brown sugar
115g/4oz/½ cup butter, softened, plus extra for greasing
50ml/2fl oz/¼ cup olive oil
3 eggs
115g/4oz/1 cup quinoa flour
75g/3oz/¾ cup ground almonds
5ml/1 tsp baking powder
2.5ml/½ tsp bicarbonate of soda (baking soda)
5ml/1 tsp ground cinnamon
2.5ml/½ tsp ground nutmeg
5ml/1 tsp vanilla extract
275g/10oz/2 cups grated carrots
50g/2oz/⅓ cup raisins
30ml/2 tbsp unsweetened cocoa powder and 4–5 squares dark (bittersweet) chocolate, to decorate

For the frosting

350g/12oz/3 cups icing (confectioners') sugar
150g/5oz/⅔ cup cream cheese
50g/2oz/¼ cups butter, softened

1 Preheat the oven to 180°C/350°F/Gas 4. Butter and line a 20cm/8in cake tin (pan).

2 In a large bowl, using an electric mixer or a hand whisk, beat together the sugar, butter and olive oil until light in colour and fluffy. Add the remaining ingredients and stir to form a batter.

3 Pour the mixture into the tin and bake for 40–50 minutes, until a skewer comes out clean. Remove from the oven and leave to stand for 10 minutes, then remove the cake from the tin and set aside to cool completely on a wire rack.

4 Make the frosting by beating together the ingredients in a bowl until smooth.

5 Decorate the cooled cake with the frosting, creating a swirled effect with the back of a fork. Sift over the cocoa powder and grate the chocolate on top.

6 Serve in slices, with a cup of coffee. The cake will keep in the refrigerator for up to a week.

Nutritional Information: Gluten free
Energy 335kcal/1397kJ; Protein 5g; Carbohydrate 33g, of which sugars 24g; Fat 21g, of which saturates 8g; Cholesterol 64mg; Calcium 59mg; Fibre 1g; Sodium 207mg.

This is a simple, quinoa-rich cookie recipe that will give you lasting satisfaction for those mid-morning or afternoon breaks. Baking time is important with these biscuits: cook them for too long and they scorch, but if you take them out of the oven too early they won't be crisp, so keep a close eye on them in the last few minutes of baking.

ORANGE QUINOA COOKIES

MAKES 18–20
250g/9oz/1⅛ cups soft butter
175g/6oz/generous 1¾ cup soft light
   brown sugar
115g/4oz/1 cup quinoa flakes
115g/4oz/1 cup quinoa flour
finely grated rind of 3 oranges

45ml/3 tbsp golden (light corn) syrup
10ml/2 tsp vanilla extract
icing (confectioners') sugar, for dusting

1 Preheat the oven to 190°C/375°F/ Gas 5. Line two large baking sheets with baking parchment.

2 With an electric mixer or a wooden spoon, beat the butter and sugar together until light and fluffy.

3 Stir in the quinoa flakes and flour with the orange rind, golden syrup and vanilla extract and combine thoroughly.

4 Place large teaspoonfuls of the mixture on the baking sheets, slightly flattening each one with the back of a damp spoon and leaving a little space for them to spread. Bake for 12–15 minutes, until golden.

5 Remove from the oven and leave on the baking trays for a few minutes before transferring to a wire rack to cool. Dust with icing sugar and serve.

VARIATION
For chocolate orange cookies, add 25g/1oz chocolate chips when you stir in the dry ingredients.

Nutritional Information per 2 cookies: Gluten free Energy 352kcal/1467kJ; Protein 4g; Carbohydrate 37g, of which sugars 22g; Fat 22g, of which saturates 14g; Cholesterol 53mg; Calcium 32mg; Fibre 1g; Sodium 168mg.

This recipe is a tasty and effective twist on traditional flapjacks. It uses quinoa flakes, which are firmer and more substantial than rolled oats, but still have a delicious gooey sweetness when cooked. These flapjacks are full of slow-release carbohydrates, and so are great for mid-morning snacks and in children's lunch boxes.

DATE AND WALNUT QUINOA FLAPJACKS

MAKES 8
115g/4oz/½ cup butter
75g/3oz/6 tbsp muscovado
   (molasses) sugar
30ml/2 tbsp golden (light corn) syrup
50g/2oz/⅓ cup dates, finely chopped
30ml/2 tbsp roughly chopped walnuts
115g/4oz/1 cup quinoa flakes
30ml/2 tbsp rolled oats
5ml/1 tsp mixed (apple pie) spice
coffee or hot chocolate, to serve

1 Preheat the oven to 200°C/400°F/Gas 6. Grease and line a 18 x 18cm/7 x 7in square baking tin (pan).

2 In a medium pan, melt the butter, sugar and golden syrup together until the butter has melted; stir to combine.

3 Add the remaining ingredients to the pan and stir well until the ingredients are completely combined.

4 Transfer the mixture into the base of the prepared tin, flattening with the back of a wooden spoon and pushing to the edges of the tin until the top is level.

5 Bake for 12–14 minutes until firm and golden brown. Score into eight slices while still warm, then leave to cool in the tin until completely cold.

6 Turn the flapjacks out of the tin. Serve with frothy coffee or hot chocolate, or store in an airtight container.

VARIATION
Replace the golden (light corn) syrup with honey, and use alternative fruit and nuts if you prefer.

....
Nutritional Information: Gluten free
Energy 255kcal/1064kJ; Protein 3g; Carbohydrate 26g, of which sugars 15g; Fat 16g, of which saturates 8g; Cholesterol 30mg; Calcium 35mg; Fibre 2g; Sodium 103mg.

Muffins are great for feeding hungry mouths at the end of the day, or between meals when a high-sugar snack would not give you the same lasting sustenance. Flaxseeds (linseeds) are a source of essential Omega 3 fats, and soluble fibre, and they work well used ground in baking because their goodness is impossible to detect.

FLAXSEED AND RAISIN QUINOA MUFFINS

MAKES 12

250ml/8fl oz/1 cup buttermilk (see Cook's tips)
150ml/¼ pint/⅔ cup vegetable oil
2 eggs
175g/6oz/1½ cups quinoa flour
115g/4oz/1 cup ground flaxseeds (linseeds)
5ml/1 tsp baking powder
5ml/1 tsp ground cinnamon
5ml/1 tsp ground nutmeg
115g/4oz/⅔ cup caster (superfine) sugar
50g/2oz/⅓ cup raisins
30ml/2 tbsp whole flaxseeds, for sprinkling
coffee, or fresh sliced banana and crème fraîche, to serve

1 Preheat the oven to 200°C/400°F/ Gas 6. Pour the buttermilk into a jug (pitcher), and beat in the oil and eggs.

2 Sift the quinoa flour into a large bowl, then stir in the ground flaxseeds, baking powder, ground cinnamon, nutmeg, sugar and raisins.

3 Make a well in the centre of the dry ingredients, then pour in the buttermilk and egg mixture, stirring briefly to just combine the ingredients. The mixture needs to be of a dropping consistency to ensure a soft crumb, so add a little extra buttermilk if required.

4 Divide the muffin mixture between 12 muffin tins (pans), lined with paper cases if you wish.

5 Sprinkle the top of each muffin with a few whole flaxseeds, and use the end of a teaspoon to push any exposed raisins into the batter if you want to avoid any scorching as they cook.

6 Bake for 18–20 minutes, until the muffins are well risen and firm to the touch. Remove from the tins and cool on a wire rack.

7 Serve warm with coffee, or with fresh sliced banana and a little crème fraîche for a tea-time treat.

COOK'S TIPS

• If you can't find buttermilk, make your own by adding 15ml/1 tbsp lemon juice to 250ml/8fl oz/1 cup full-fat (whole) milk. Leave to stand for 5 minutes, after which it will be ready to use as buttermilk.
• It is easy to grind flaxseeds yourself in a coffee bean grinder or food processor. Store in an airtight container. It is thought that the nutritious properties of the seeds are only properly released when ground.

Nutritional Information per muffin: Gluten free Energy 287kcal/1197kJ; Protein 6g; Carbohydrate 25g, of which sugars 14g; Fat 19g, of which saturates 3g; Cholesterol 23mg; Calcium 51mg; Fibre 2g; Sodium 24mg.

INDEX